The Power of Peace

New Perspectives in Lao Tzu's Tao Te Ching

Translated with Commentary

by

Thomas Early

DEDICATION

This book is dedicated to President Jimmy Carter,
tireless worker for peace and a true man of practical faith.

An explanation of the characters on the front cover

The two Chinese characters on the front cover are CHANG, upper
and TAO, lower. CHANG can mean universal or common; also
absolute, ultimate, eternal. I have translated it as extra-ordinary.
TAO can mean at once, path, way, word, doctrine, insight. CHANG
TAO: the extra-ordinary way. Lao Tsu warns us that all verbal
expressions of TAO are futile. It's the way things are.

CONTENTS

Part Three: The Way of the People

Jottings On The Way To Peace

ACKNOWLEDGMENTS

I would like to thank family, friends, colleagues, and students for their encouragement and suggestions in progress of this project. I'd like to express my gratitude to Gary Bloomfield for his artistry in creating the designs and graphics for the cover. Special thanks are due to my editor and publisher, Michael Furniss of Wild Earth Press for continuing his deft navigating through the currents of modern publishing and realizing this work. Probably even more important is his role in what Aristotle would call the energizing factor and agent cause in jump-starting this incarnation of Lao Tzu.

Who is Lao Tzu: A Historical Note

The Quest for the Historical Lao Tzu is fraught with difficulty. On one hand there is a component of legend, myth and symbol. On the other is the search for factual data, which is extremely scarce. Conclusions vary from, "Lao Tzu never existed" to his miraculous birth as a fully-formed sage, born of a shooting star.

Perhaps it is best to follow Plato's rule when you have a mix of universes of discourse: To use what Plato calls, "A likely story" or "Plausible account", reconstructed from the different levels of meaning and evidence. Something like this: In the middle of the Sixth Century B.C., a scholar-sage appeared named Master Lao. He gathered around himself a group of followers.

Disenchanted with the political situation in his region, Master Lao climbed on the back of a water buffalo and wandered into the motherland of Northwestern China. Persuaded by a gatekeeper to leave behind some of the wisdom, he wrote down 81 poems and then he disappeared.

It is not known how the disciples received a copy of the text. It certainly has been amended, but as with any ancient text, the kernels are there, and the inspired disciples embellished them in the spirit of the original.

What we have is a text, the Lao Tzu Tao Te Ching. In a sense the details of his life do not matter. The text is there for our enlightened practice. Whoever Lao Tzu was, his influence continues today. The focus of this translation is walking the peaceful path, which is not passive.

It is my humble hope that I can map a few footprints along that path that might be useful to the modern reader.

Note on Theme and Format

What keynotes this collection is a completely new format oriented around a fourfold strategy for "recovering the root" of peace in oneself, the community, and nature. The eighty-one poems are now divided almost equally into several directions on the way to peace:

I. The Way of Peace in the Politics of Living
The insight here is that properly understood, power and success in the inescapable community of things are ultimately realized through a non-aggressive and non-violent approach.

II. The Way of the Leader
Power is a matter of centering and channelling. The key here is low profile, a light touch, a pure heart, and wide-angled vision.

III. The Way of the People
The basic qualities to cultivate are: simplicity, honesty, sharing, flexibility, openness, and compassion.

IV. The Way of the Way
All in All, peace is the norm. Common and rarefied, inexpressible and everpresent, easy and simple, it eludes one's grasp; it's the Way Things Are.

PART ONE:

THE WAY OF PEACE
IN THE POLITICS OF LIVING

Poem Nine

SIMPLER MEANS, HIGHER ENDS

To press or stretch a thing
Beyond its bounds
Is time ill-spent.

To temper and hone a sword
Beyond the edge of sense
Is dull-witted indeed.

Halls filled full
With guns and gold
Have no defense.

Thus pride of stealth or wealth
Brings on its own misfortune.
So whatever fate or fame
May follow deeds done,
The sage proceeds
Along a higher Way.

Poem Twenty-Three

TAKING LIFE AT ITS WORD

All in all
Stillness is the norm.
The rudest winds
Are quite soon spent;
And torrential rains
Prevail at most a day.

So even nature
When aroused, lets up.
So much the more
Should it be for
Humbler human powers.

Take life as it comes your way---
Be one with it.
Seek life's wild finesse
And become as deliberate
And refined as creation's
Simplest work.

Find fault and you will tend
To fail yourself.
So rejoice in taking
Life at its word,
Attending nature's gentle power
With calm delight.

To dwell on a moment's loss
Is the self's indulgent blindness
To the wider wonders that be.
Trust life
And it will entrust
Itself to you.

Poem Twenty-Six

MASTER THE SELF

MIND WHAT MATTERS

GO IN PEACE

As momentous things
May proceed with grace,
And life's furious pace
May flurry about
Like a winter's snow,

So sages travel on and on
Bearing their burdens lightly,
Taking dazzling vistas
In their stride.

Why then do those whose will
Commands ten thousand chariots
Become so slight of soul
That their realm
Slips out of hand
And confusion takes the reins?

Poem Twenty-Nine

DON'T MESS WITH HEAVEN'S TOOLS

One sees how power-hungry souls
Obsessed with molding
The world to their will
Seldom succeed for long.
The world is a sacred vessel
To be handled with a light
And reverent touch.
Clutch its power
And it will elude you.

Some are meant to lead,
Others to follow;
Some to gain,
Others to lose;
Some to be firm and strong,
Others infirm and frail;
Some to achieve,
Others to fail.

Therefore, sages avoid
Extremes of passion--
Indeed, all indulgence of the self--
And pursue the good and simple life
Without extravagance.

Poem Thirty

THE WAYWARD PATH HASTENS TO ITS END

The right way to help
The guardians of the people
Is to develop their power to serve
Without force of arms,
And to conduct all business
In good faith.

What else but briars and thorns
Will grow in armed encampments?
What meager harvests rise
From former battlegrounds!

Just rulers are content
With what brings forth good fruit
Without need to force its growth
Or seize the harvest for private gain.

The wise propose without imposing,
Persist without presumption,
Prevail without seeking glory.
Firmness sparingly applied
Succeeds without violence.

Force the fruit
And hasten decay--
Push the river
And be carried away!

Poem Thirty-One

SHUN THE UNHAPPY USES OF WAR

Fine weapons are misfortunes' tools--
A dread to the fit and sane.
Those who keep to The Way
Barely abide their use.
Wise rulers cherish peacefulness
Within their realm--
And far beyond as well.

When forced to fight
The sage gives arms their necessary place.
Yet these harsh devices
Are not the stock-in-trade
Of just leaders who
Procure and use them
Only as a last resort.

Peace and gentleness are valued most
By sages who savor not
The taste of victory.
Those who revel in it
Are celebrating murder!
How do people who trade in death
Ever get their way in the world?

Perhaps in good times
We should honor the peacemakers,
Giving the military second place.
In times of conflict
We should respect the courageous
And so give generals their due...
With all the ceremony of a funeral.
Bewailing the senseless waste of war,
We chant our triumphs with a dirge.

Poem Thirty-Three

HOW GOOD TRANFSORMS THE SELF

Prudence searches others,
But wisdom finds the self.
Force may conquer others,
Where goodness transfigures life.

Know the treasures of contentment;
Persevere and brace your step.
Being at home in all the world,
You outlast the longest journey,
Finding death is but
A wayside inn.

Poem Thirty-Six

AN OPEN SECRET

Things about to fold
Began by standing up.
Diminishing returns of power
At first gave back in ample measure.
What's ruined once had flourished.
The deprived were once
Quite generously set.

Recall this subtle insight into life:
The soft and pliant overcome
The stiff and tough.
But just as fish cannot escape
The sea's dark depth,
So this insight into tools of state
Dawns on people far too late.

Poem Forty-Two

THE WAY OF GENESIS

Creation's Way
Is to emerge all at once
As a single breath of life--
A primal unity of spirit.
It then unfolds in two-fold power,
Yin and Yang,
Whose offspring humankind
Must hold in loving custody,
Creation's garden
Of ten thousand things.

All the world depends on Yin:
The dark, devoted, feminine, the ever-
Receptive field of energy and matter,
Nurture holding sway.
All embrace the equal power of Yang:
The masculine delight in form
And firmness directing the creative
Patterns of the world.
All vital force is the primal
Union of these two powers.

Coming down to earth
From such metaphysical flights--
One would guess there might
Be something to it when
Royalty pretend such worthy titles
As "Homeless Waif,"
Or "Homely Widow."

In just such ways
Initial lack may come to gain,

Or early lead may turn up last.
I, too, expound the old saying that
Unyielding and aggressive souls
Endure unseemly death.
I take this to be
My most basic teaching.

Poem Forty-Three

HOW THE YIELDING WAY WINS IN THE END

What opens up the most
And yields way
In the course of life,
Runs circles round
The rigid powers that be.
The unassuming find their way
Into the most exclusive places.

So one finds advantage
In making no fuss,
And getting the point across
By keeping still.
How few, in the busy-ness
Of the world
Profit by this insight!

Poem Forty-Six

CURB DESIRE AND BE CONTENT

The world is truly on the right road
When its trucks haul compost
And not devices of death
Along the wayward path of war.

There is no greater misdeed
Than misspent passion;
No greater misfortune
Than lasting discontent,
Or quiet desperation;
No greater evil than
Desire for selfish gain.

It's better to see how much
Life simply holds in store
And so be ever content
Along the tranquil Way.

Poem Fifty-Seven

KEEP IT CALM AND SIMPLE AND AVOID THE FUSS

A nation is the rule of ordinary ends;
An army, the school of extraordinary means.
But nature has no truck with either tool.
How do I know the world to be so?
This is the way all things must go!

In the world,
As rules begin to multiply,
More people end up with empty plates.
When the masses race to gather guns,
Delusion reigns as law and order
Ascend the throne, while
Thieves and brigands outnumber
Officers of uneasy peace.

Sagely counsel points out the way:
With less to do,
The people transform themselves.
With the habit of tranquility
They find the right path on their own.
With fewer meddling eyes and greedy hands,
The true wealth of a nation
Flourishes of itself.

By checking passion's reckless flow
The people take a simpler road.

Poem Sixty-Six

THE LOWLY ROAD TO THE HIGHER GOOD

Great rivers and seas prevail
Over the waters of the earth
Because they gather in
The lowest places in the land
As all currents are naturally
Drawn to them.

So sages preside over people
With humble speech;
Provide for others
Putting self behind.

Since their surpassing life
Is hardly a burden to the people,
And their abiding care
Leaves no trace of harm,
The world rejoices to exalt them,
And neither ruler nor
The ruled grows weary.

Poem Sixty-Eight

A PERFECT MATCH FOR HEAVEN

The best warrior is most unwarlike--
Fighting without anger.
In the fairest fight
The foe is won over
Without a contest.

When it comes to other
Fields of contention,
One finds superior service
In a nation whose leaders
Put the people first.

Such is the power
In avoiding strife--
People working at their best.

A worthy match for heaven,
As the ancients say,
Life at the utmost along The Way.

Poem Sixty-Nine

ADVANCE BY WITHDRAWING
PREVAIL BY YIELDING

It is said in strategies of war
Not to venture being host,
But rather play the guest.
It is better to withdraw a foot
And with the greatest caution
Inch one's way ahead.

This is how to advance
With the slightest step
And leave no track,
Clear the way without a sword,
Proceed with no resistance,
And prevail without force.

The height of misfortune
Is to take your match
Too lightly and measure
By loss whatever you've gained.

With those dead set
On a headstrong fray,
Only the yielding
Will win the day.

Poem Seventy-Three

DARING TO DIE AND DARING TO LIVE

Boldness takes the risk of death;
Courage takes the risk of life.
Either one may suffer
Gain or loss.
Who knows why we fall
From heaven's favor?
For even sages wonder
At fortune's turning.

Heaven's way does not contend,
Yet carries the day;
Speaks no word,
But finds response;
Without commanding,
Draws all to hand;
Works out its plan
With infinite patience.
So vast is heaven's net
It gathers all in its
Measureless span.

Poem Seventy-Four

STANDING IN FOR THE GREAT CARPENTER

When people lose
Their fear of death
What ghosts are there
To frighten them?

Yet when we hold
The threat of death
Over breakers of the law,
Who presumes to seize
And kill such wayward ones?

Those who stand in nature's place
In executing higher laws
May find themselves
Cut off along the way.

The artless use of sharp devices
Seldom yields but shreds and slices!

Poem Seventy-Eight

NOTHING SURPASSES THE WAY OF WATER

What in the world
Among the soft and yielding
Could surpass the subtle power
Of water as it works its way
On the hard and strong?

None can take its place
As it prevails by yielding.
All that is firm gives way
Indeed to the gentle play
Of weaker forces.

The world finds this truth
Too obvious to take to task.
So the wise endure
In peace the world's ill will,
And bear with its misfortune.

Yet somehow these sages
Command a higher grace
While bound to life's highest post.
This paradox is
In truth their fate.

Poem Seventy-Nine

HEAVEN HELPS THE SPIRITUALLY FIT

Even if one could ease
Contending forces
A bitter discontent
Remains to plague
The powers that work for good.

The sagely way accepts
The short end and
Makes no claim on others.
The wise work with skill
On the task at hand.
The fool holds back
And makes demands.

Though they seek no favors
On the Sacred Way,
Sages find the yoke is easy
And the burden light.

Poem Eighty-One

A BLESSED AND ABUNDANT YIELD
ALONG THE SACRED WAY

Sound words may not compare
With fairer turns of phrase
That put a mask on truth.
So better be
The uncontending one,
Silent in your wisdom,
Than play the fool who,
In the know, goes on and on.

Take the sagely Way
And gather as you go
The measure of labor's
Love for others.
How blest you are
When people grow
From what you give.

What treasures grace
The Sacred Path
As misfortune turns away.
The wise contend with nothing,
And go about their work
Along The Way.

PART TWO:

THE WAY OF THE LEADER

Poem Three

NOTHING TOO WORTHY
NOTHING UNRULY

Don't raise up the worthy
Then the people stay unwrangled.
Put no stock in precious goods,
And they won't be led to plunder.
Seeing nothing to desire,
The heart keeps unentangled.

Thus the yield of a sagely rule:

Hearts made pure,
Desires quenched.
Wills becalmed,
Frames made firm.

Not nurturing people's wants and wiles
Keeps the cunning from their craft.
If you preside without force or fuss
Things find the measure of themselves.

Poem Ten

FLAWLESS POWER

Is it in the power
Of your earthbound soul
To remain whole
And not be scattered?
Can the strength
Of your vital spirit
Be pliant as an infant?
Are the lenses
Of your inward eye
Kept open, clean,
And flawless?

A realm where selfless love
Becomes the norm
Leaves no place
For guile or force.

As heaven unveils
The given forms of things
Can you devoutly keep
The vision clear,
Encompassing all,
Avoiding vain pretense
Or blind misuse?

Can you help the people grow,
Unfettered, self-reliant,
Raised without a lash or leash?
Such good, in fact,
Unlocks life's creative power.

Poem Sixteen

RECOVERING OUR ROOTS

Reach for the higher
Mountain places of your self
All calm and clear
And see
How all things rise
To flourish and return--
Each creature coming home
To recover its roots.

Recovering the root
Means just this:
The dynamics of peace
By being recalled
To our common fate
In the kinship of all creation.

Knowing this eternal truth
One sees all things with
Extraordinary clarity--
Eternity's radiant light.
Blind to this truth
Leaders sow the seeds
Of reckless deeds and
Their evil fruits.

But when rulers plant
By this constant star
They embrace the world
And serve it fairly,
Guiding people
On the Celestial Path,
Who fearless pass Death's Gate
On the Everlasting Way.

Poem Seventeen

ACHIEVING SELF-RELIANCE

Great rulers are scarcely known--
For people tend to find
The second rate to praise,
The third rate to fear,
The fourth rate to despise.

So as dishonest rulers
Foment mistrust,
Beware of fine-sounding words
And rather let merit
Attend what matters at hand.
People then will take
Their own and others'
Success in stride.

Poem Eighteen

LOSING THE WAY

When the Great Way is lost
A realm resorts to benevolence
And then upholds
Mere righteous self respect.

What follows is a bootstrap prudence
With a glaze of pedantry.
It all adds up to
Common cunning in the end.

Such is the ruinous road
Of lesser virtues leading on
To vain pretense and discord
Among the people.

What's left to rule are
Family ties and the sentiment of
Mere duty as the country
Dwells in dark confusion.

The birth of chaos
Is the death of a people
Led by fawning sheep
Who've lost The Way.

Poem Twenty-Seven

UNCOMMON GOODNESS
IS THE HABIT OF ENLIGHTENMENT

Note well how
Good moves avoid ruts,
Good speech is free
Of flaw or blame,
Good plans by-pass red tape,
Good doors need
Neither lock nor key,
Yet no thief can open them.
Imagine bonds so sure
And firm that rope and chains
Are superfluous,
Yet no one can unfasten them.

In just this way
Uncommon goodness in the sage
Serves each and all
Exceptionally well,
Saving things for use
And wasting nothing.

This habit of enlightenment
Is what makes the sage so fit
To guide the unwary and unwise.
Folks less fit are
The necessary trust for
The sage's work and keep.

Not to cherish these guides
Nor love their charges
Is the great delusion
Of the cunning soul.
For the guardian's truth
Is the very bond of spirit.

Poem Twenty-Eight

RETURN TO THE SIMPLE

To face the adventure of your life
With creative courage
Yet maintain a spirit
Of humble nurture,
Simply sustain the world
In its course as if
You were its valley.
Conduct the living stream
This natural Way and so
Recover that extraordinary
Freshness and fitness of a child.

In such youthful wonder
One may behold the clear and
Brilliant face of things
To fearlessly embrace the dark
And teeming world around.
From this calm and simple bearing
The sage transforms the world
With a skill uncommon
And unfailing, and so
Becomes the world's measure
By recovering life's infinite
Reserve of spiritual Power.

Knowing their own best lights
Sages always put others first
As they help and guide the people.
By following the natural flow
Of things, sages tap the deep
And constant source of strength.
Relying on the basic integrity of life

They handle each task with ease and care.
In the sway of peaceful wisdom
True guardians of state are few but first rate.
That's how a sagely ruler
Avoids the cut of chaos
And the wayward winds of war.

Poem Thirty-Two

NATURE'S BALANCE

No words convey
The everlasting Way of Life.
Though extraordinarily plain and simple,
Nothing in the world can conquer it.

But if rulers could abide by it,
The world's homage would be theirs.
Sweet and gentle rains would fall
On a land united.

Balance and order would reign
Among the people.
A country's only ruler would be
A natural equity shared by all.

But with the rise of civil order
Came laws and norms
With their class distinctions
And endless regulations.
What leader knows how to stop it?

One who sees
True power in The Way
Varied streams and rivers
Flow toward one
Great Sea.

Poem Thirty-Four

PERFECTING LIFE WITH NO EFFORT

Can one direct the course
Of life's great tide?
Indeed, this universal flood
Sustains and nurtures
All creation without fail.

One marvels at the way
This sea completes its task
But takes no honors.
With loving care it raises
Every creature without
A dominating hand.

Because it transcends
The narrower currents of desire,
The ocean's power works simply
And with subtle and mass effects.

All things rise and recede
With life's ocean swell;
Just so, the grand tide of life
Claims nothing for itself.
In this its greatness lies.

Poem Thirty-Seven

A SIMPLE CHANGE

The true Way of Life
Does all things with little to do.
If rulers would abide by this,
All the world would transform itself.

When people's channels of desire
Rise up and rage,
One directs them through
The nameless simplicity of nature.

In plain truth
The simple Way of Life,
Free from the clutch
Of unbridled passion,
Keeps calm and clear.

In nature
Peace prevails
In due course.

Poem Thirty-Nine

GETTING TO THE ROOT OF INTEGRITY

The oneness of the creative
Scheme of heaven
Lends clarity and direction
To all that exists.
The oneness of the devoted
Receptive earth
Provides a tranquil field
For creation's work.
The oneness of the spiritual realm
Brings depth into the world.

Integrity in a well
Assures its fullness.
The integrity of any creature
Is what gives it life
And makes it fruitful.
Just as integrity in a ruler
Sets the measure of
The world's peace and plenty,
So all these things are what they are
By virtue of their wholeness.

Lacking clarity, the heavenly order
Would be torn asunder.
Lacking peaceful balance,
The earth would split apart.
Without refreshing winds
From the spiritual plane,
All life would soon expire.
Wells half full may soon go dry.
Creatures lacking vital strength
Soon perish and become extinct.

Rulers losing the measured
Integrity of The Way
Stumble on the path to
Infamy or dark oblivion.
In light of this, note well
How true nobility is rooted
In common clay; and how
The exalted have the humble
As their foundation.

What's behind the mask
The world's worthies wear--
Affecting peasant roots,
Rubbing shoulders with the masses?
What good is the carriage of state
Without its wheel?
Respectability still bears
The jangle of jade
Where true humility prefers
The sound of simpler stones.

Poem Forty-Eight

THE USE OF SELFLESS SERVICE

Tend your lessons daily
And your ego gains.
Attend the Way of Life
And your ego daily lessens,
'Til such diminishing
Returns your ego
To a less imposing state,
Freeing your self
To accomplish everything
With little to do.

The greatest masters
Rule vast realms
As dispassionate servants,
While those whose unruly passion
Is to take the world by storm
Are unfit to serve even themselves.

Poem Forty-Nine

THE WORKINGS OF A GREAT
AND TRUSTING HEART

Sages lack the common sway
Of heart and mind, and so
They manage all the people's needs
In an unbiased way.

Good and bad alike
Are treated with equal fairness
As befits the workings of
A higher spirit.

Sincere and insincere
Are taken in good faith;
For such is the sacred trust
Of sagely power.

Thus, these holy ones
In awe of the world,
Work their way as if bemused.
Yet the eyes and ears of nations
Wait upon these humble souls
Who treat the people as their family.

Poem Fifty-Eight

THE GENTLE AND GENEROUS HEART

Rule in a lower key
Will keep simplicity
Among the people.
Raise the pitch of
Meddlesome means and
People's need increases.

Weal and woe take their turns
On fortune's road--
Each leading on and
Hiding from each other.
Who knows this circle's end?
When exceptions become the rule
And evil measures out the goods,
Confusion reigns among the people.

How does a sage set right
A world on end?
By being
Just but not fierce,
Frugal without cutting corners,
Direct but not blunt.
The sage has the light
To show The Way
Without self-glory.

Poem Fifty-Nine

NATURE'S POWER:
THE HABIT OF RESOURCEFULNESS

When it comes to ruling people
And tending the Celestial Way
Nothing surpasses conserving
Force and resource.

Such sparing ways simply mean
Having foresight to gather and store
Life's Power through which
All things are possible.

Only one in whom the Power of
Goodness is natural,
Boundless, and irresistible,
Is truly fit to rule the realm.

When nature's balance
Is the mother of a people,
They endure.
The tree of community
Deeply planted,
Growing strong
Will stand forever
In the light of The Way.

Poem Sixty

RECOVERING THE NATURAL COMMUNITY OF PEOPLE

Rule a great state with a light touch.
For a nation guided in such a way
Is unspooked by political ghosts.

If rulers take the sagely Path
They bring no sorrow to the people
Who return no grief in kind.

Indeed, true Power
Resides in recovering
The living spirit
Of community.

Poem Sixty-One

THE QUIET FLOW OF POWER

Like a vast sea
Toward which the world's waters
Flow and join
A great nation receives the world
As a devoted wife,
Mastering her mate's advances
By her calm centeredness.
For by supporting the inferior
Great nations hold sway,
Just as smaller states, by adapting,
Draw power from the strong.

As the great may yield to gain,
So the lowly offers to serve--
Both are winners in this game.
As larger states need mainly
Feed and harmonize their own,
Sharing surplus,
So smaller nations go out
To serve themselves and others.
Each thus will get its fill.
For power gains its highest yield
By the giving and opening Way.

Poem Sixty-Five

BLESSED ARE THE PURE IN HEART FOR THEY SHALL RETURN ON THE RADIANT WAY

Those of old who mastered
The Way of Life
Did not attempt
To enlighten the people.
They only sought to preserve
The natural simplicity of living.
For when shrewdness is the rule,
The people are unruly.
When leaders preside with cunning,
The land is cursed and barren.

Blessed is the land
Where wisdom reigns,
Whose guardians heed the signs
Of woe and blessing,
Who mark the path
And lead The Way.
To rule in such wise
Is to tap the depths of Power
Flowing clear,
Running true,
And reaching far.
All life prospers when
The spirit of true community
Returns to favor all
Who dwell in the natural Way.

Poem Seventy-Two

THE FULL MEASURE OF ONE'S DEVOTION

The advent of misfortune
Is signalled by a general
Irreverence pointing to
Oppressive rule,
Contracted leisure, and
Wearisome work.

Overburdened people find
Their leaders an early retirement.
So wise rulers keep clear their vision
But avoid a vain display,
Regard themselves as dispensible,
And so stand firm in the power
Of their inner worth.
They prevail in the outer world
Giving in the way of earth.

Poem Seventy-Five

THE GOOD LIFE MAKES LIGHT OF DEATH

Consumed by taxes
To fatten the rich
People starve and
Become unruly.

As their leaders
Meddle all the more,
Things only grow worse.
For death rests lightly
On those weighed down
By the cares of life.

For what it's worth,
The rich or poor less bent
On the good life
May simply find themselves
More content along The Way.

Poem Seventy-Seven

SERVING THE WORLD IN THE WAY OF HEAVEN

The Way of Life
On heaven's path
Is like the drawing of a bow:
The long ends shorten
As tension and width increase.

Just so, creation's Sacred Way
Fulfills what lacks by
Drawing on the well-supplied
To make all things complete
In perfect balance.

The human way turns things around
Reducing even more
The wanting side to glut
The selfish hide of those
Who already have too much.

Who but those who take
The sagely Way possess
An inward treasure and so
Can truly serve the world.

So sages act
But make no claim;
Complete all tasks
Without dwelling on their success;
Do each thing
In a surpassing way
Without the least desire
For vain display.

Poem Eighty

NO PLACE TO VISIT: OR THE DIMINISHED RETURNS

Better to keep
Your country small
Your people few
Your devices simple--
And even those for
Infrequent use.

Let people measure life
By the meaning of death
And not go out of their way
To visit far off places.
With nowhere to travel
And little care for display,
Great ships, fine carriages,
And shining weapons become
Mere relics of the past.

Let people recover
The simple life:
Reckoning by knotted cords,
Delighting in a basic meal,
Pleased with humble attire,
Happy in their homes,
Taking pleasure in their
Rustic ways.

So content are they
That in nearby towns--
So close the sound
Of dogs and roosters
Forms one chorus--
Folks grown gray with age
May pass away never having
Strayed beyond their village.

PART THREE:

THE WAY OF THE PEOPLE

Poem Two

THE INTERPLAY OF BEING AND ITS SHADOW

Unable to see the good and fair
For what they are,
People set fixed norms,
Confusing effect for inner worth,
As they proscribe all sorts of
"Bad and ugly" things which
May not really be so.
From failing inner vision
They miss the interplay of
Existence and its shadow--

How distress and ease
Are phases in one work;
That what's long or short on skill
Are measured by a common task;
Why the high and lowly
Take each other's place;
That tone and pitch
Unite in single sound;
And what stays behind
May really lead the way.

Accordingly, the sage
Attends to tasks without a fuss,
Instructs without a sermon,
Affirms all things as they arise,
Nurtures each but shuns possession,
Works without demand or claim,
Succeeds but doesn't dwell on it.
By not relying or gloating
On past success, the sage abides
With things along The Way.

Poem Eight

IN DUE SEASON

The highest good,
Like water,
Will nourish all things
Without undue resistance.
It abides in places
Most folks shun,
As streams will flow unseen
And nearest to the common course--
So things run by nature.

When people, calm and
Deliberate as the turning sky,
Choose a solid house,
Compassionate thoughts,
Truthful words,
Competent rule,
They recover
A higher fitness
In all life's affairs,
Attending to
Good timing with
The work at hand.

Just so, the sagely Way
Serves like water
Flowing beneath the fray
And skirting fault or blame.

Poem Twelve

KEEPING TO THE INWARD PATH

As too many colors
May trick the eye,
Or too much noise
Confuse the ear,
Or too many flavors
Can jade one's taste,

And just as the race
And the mad dash hunt
Make the mind go mad,
And straining for riches
Takes the fun out of life,

So sages select and attend
The more inward than
Outward side of things
And finally come to their senses.

Poem Thirteen

HIGH ANXIETY

In or out of grace
Beware!
As a fortune made
Or missed is
Largely ego's trick.

Just what are these
Fateful graces
Good or bad?
For services rendered
Often rue the favored
More than those denied.
Again, beware of both.

So what is meant by saying
These inflated goods
And empty griefs
Are ego's game?
Just that our
Greatest cares
Are born of a small,
Possessive self.

So rise above yourself--
Be free of worry and woe!
Only those who care
For the world
As their widest self
May live and hold
The world in trust.

Poem Fifteen

THE OLD FASHIONED WAY TO BE NEW

The wise of old
Were fine spiritual masters
Whose profound vision
Cannot be known
Through learning.
Yet though such sages
Can't be tackled in the
Common pedant's way,
One draws them out
Perhaps like this:

Deliberate
When wading winter streams,
Careful
Of surrounding dangers,
Reserved
As a grateful guest,
Yielding
As melting ice,
Simple and unassuming
As uncarved wood,
Open and obliging
As a mountain vale,
Obscure
As turbid water.

Who can render pure and calm
Life's muddy torrent?
Or nurture growth
From a quiet center,
Moving mountains
In the simplest style?

Those who trust The Way, of course!
Unconcerned with fulfillment,
Sages never overfill their day
And flourish in gray old age
Making life's late season
More like spring.

Poem Nineteen

PLAIN AND SIMPLE

Rid of pedantry and prudence
The people gain a hundredfold.
Spared the high hand of benevolence
And the airs of upright souls
Folks recover the more
Natural bonds of human kindness.
Void of cunning means and ways,
Renouncing private gain,
The people are no longer prey
To thieves and other malcontents.

Yet all this falls short of true culture.
In genuine community
People stick to what's reliable:

>   Finding simple ways
>   Embracing honest means
>   Limiting personal claims
>   Checking passion's flow.

Poem Twenty

CAREFREE AND LIVING FROM NATURE

Better to be ignorant and unconcerned
With the stickler's fuss about
"like and dislike," or "good and bad."
Best to avoid the endless tangles over
What to fear and not to.

As low or highborn folks will
Revel in their joys
As at a feast, their spirits soaring
Like the quickening air of spring,
The sage alone remains at ease
And uninvolved,
Like a child too young to smile
And wandering homeless.

As the people more than take their fill,
The sage, a fool at heart,
Gets by with little.
Bemused and overshadowed
By the world's display,
Confused by common cunning,
Such souls seem lost at sea,
Bereft of port or anchor.

Yet, while the world
Wanders busily astray,
These alone in their sagely play,
Like awkward rustics with
Outlandish ways, prefer to
Live from nature.

Poem Twenty-Two

BE OPEN AND YIELD TO PERFECTION

Yield and be whole.
Go round the circle,
Yet reach the middle too.
Be open and fulfilled;
Be weary but soon recover;
For, wanting little,
You have enough,
Unconfounded by excess.

So sages embrace a singleness
Of purpose on their way,
And find themselves
The model for the world.
Wearing the quiet habit of truth
Their beauty glows;
Light of heart and hand
Quite simply they succeed.
Hence, the yield of wholeness
And the whole point of yielding...
Which goes without saying.

Poem Twenty-Four

A FOOL'S VAIN SHOW

Those who take themselves
Too seriously tend to
Overreach and topple,
Overbear and stumble,
Showing off the
Dark and dreary play
In which they live.

Such bravado hides
An ugly life--
A braggart thinly masking
An empty part,
A stand-in crying over
Missed chances.

Such a fool's excess
Is so much litter
On life's road,
An embarrassment to all.
Those bound for higher parts
Move steadily on their Way.

Poem Thirty-Five

GOING IN STYLE!

Behold the Extraordinary Way
Life transforms itself!
Go forth before the world's wonders
Untouched, contented,
At ease in the extravagance
Of peace.

Fine food and music
Are but passing fancies.
Yet people often stop too long
To tease and sate their taste.
To them the simpler fare
Along The Way
May seem too plain,
Lacking savor to the tongue,
Dazzle for the eye, or
Splendor in the ear.

Yet the smallest wonders
On the sage's Path
Work with undiminished effect.

Poem Thirty-Eight

LOSING THE WAY AND ITS POWER

True spiritual power
Is not self-righteous,
And so conducts the powers for good
By merely being and doing.
The spiritually unfit,
Still self-conscious of their own goodness,
Lose the better part of themselves
And often work with ill effect.

The truly good
Make no fuss and act
Without pretense;
Where do-gooders act
From ego, producing
Virtue's fluff.

The truly caring
Act from self,
But without display.
The truly just
Act from self
And for themselves as well.
The truly proper ego
May behave quite in form,
But gets a blank response,
Needing strong-arm tactics
To force the issue of its will.

Thus we see how,
Losing the natural Way,
We rely on spiritual Fitness,
Regressing to the kindly way,

Then contrive the just way,
And finally react in a merely proper way.

This last resort of
Acting in proper form
Wears the thinnest mask of
Integrity and trust, and
Becomes a source of
Moral confusion and decay.

Now prophets and fortune tellers
May see the flowers of fate
Along the path, but end up sowing
Tangled weeds of foolishness.
So the noble soul abides
With important matters at hand
And doesn't dwell on superficial things.
The sage enjoys the blossom,
But attends to the harvest.

Humble masters of the art of life,
These uncontentious spirits
Remain at peace with the world.
The ancient saying,
"Yield to The Way and perfect the day,"
Is more than empty wind.
For opening and yielding is the Way
To recover true wholeness.

Poem Forty-Four

CONTENTMENT IS THE KEY TO GROWTH AND ENDURANCE

Which is your most kindred self:
Your frame or your fame?
What counts more in loss or gain:
Your wealth or health?
In losing, which causes the greatest pain?

Consider, then, these sayings:
Love over-extended
Is life soon expended.
Over-full coffers
Promise great losses.

So one finds that
The highest grace is
To be content with less.
The lowest risk is
To know when to stop.
This is the secret
Of growth and endurance.

Poem Fifty

DEATH MEANS COMING HOME TO LIFE'S ADVENTURE

In the natural way of things
All must go forth in living
And must come home in dying.
Yet as many madly run toward death
As madly serve their blind desires--
With souls of equal number
Already stuck to the quick
In the mud of their grave.

What are we to make of this awful waste?
Perhaps it's just decaying fruit
On the wayward path of self-indulgence.
Still, one hears of those who
Fair quite well on life's journey,
Fending off fierce tigers,
Wild buffalo, and armed warriors
Wilder yet.

For those who walk
The Way of Life
Provide no place
For a buffalo's horns
Or a tiger's claws
Or a soldiers sword.
How can this be?
Sages give no ground to death.

Poem Fifty-Three

BEWARD THE PRIMROSE PATH ALONG THE WAY

It only takes a little insight
To walk in the Great Way.
But beware!
The Way is so simple
People somehow prefer to wander
Off the Path.

Behold how splendid palaces
Look out on neglected fields
And empty silos.
Donning gaudy clothes and baubles,
Flashing well-honed swords,
The gentry take their glut
Of food and drink.
Excess of wealth
Is a brigand's boast--
A wayward path, indeed!

Poem Fifty-Four

DRAWING ON INFINITE POWER

Just as the firmly set stays put,
And the well-kept stays fit,
So clear-headed descendants
Honor their forbears
Who never ceased to cultivate
The true Way Of Life.
Putting its powers to the test
Is what brings out your truth.

Its Power nurtured in the family
Yields the warmth and joy
Of abundant life.
Its Power working in community
Makes way for growth more lasting
And effective in a wider sphere.
Its Power fostered in the nation
Sustains the golden horn of plenty.
Its Power spread throughout the world
Is boundless resource gracing every table.

Thus is each dimension measured
In its own domain,
Person by person,
Clan by clan,
Town by town,
Nation by nation,
And the world, too,
In its encompassing sphere.

How do I know
The world to be so?
This is The Way
All things tend
To flow.

Poem Fifty-Five

A CHILD'S GRACE ILLUMINES THE WAY

Blessed as a child are those
Who hold life's natural Power
With an easy grace.
Wild beasts won't seize them,
Birds of prey stay clear
And fly away.

Though pliant of bone
And soft of muscle,
A child's grasp is firm.
Oblivious to gender,
Its vital energy can
Grow to perfection.
Crying and sobbing all day
Without getting hoarse,
A baby keeps its own kind of balance
And lives in a world
Complete in itself.

To reach this child-like harmony
Is to recover life's extraordinariness
With radiant clarity.
Yet how many entangled souls call
Indulgence, blessing;
Willfulness, power!
Wandering these overgrown
Brambles of death in life
One misses the path
And loses The Way.

Poem Fifty-Six

GUARD THE GATES AND GATHER YOUR SELF

The wise abide in silence
The endless verbal play of others.
They master the gates of passion
And guard the doors of expression.

Their subtle powers
Dull life's daggers,
Unfasten fetters,
Tone down the glare,
And temper the pace of
The fast-shuffling world.

Such is how all things work together
In the domain of wisdom.
Beyond the reach of
Love and hate,
Gain or loss,
Praise or blame,
The sagely Way becomes
The measure of the world.

Poem Sixty-Two

FINDING YOUR WAY

All things find their niche
Along The Way:
Treasure for the good,
Shelter for the wayward.
One way or another
Clear words will gain fair trade;
Kind deeds bring grace
To someone's world.

Why should those who stray
From the Path be cast away?
So before the crowning of a queen
Or the installing of her ministers,
Let others beseech with
Gifts of jade or teams of horses,
While you come calmly forth
To offer only The Way.

The true Path of Life
Was a treasure to the ancients.
Have we not been told that
Those who seek will find and
Those who stray are spared?
This is how to measure
The world on its Way.

Poem Sixty-Three

DOING WONDERS WITH EASE

Act without fuss,
Serve without effort,
Savor without excess,
Exalt the lowly,
Provide for the needy,
Respond to hate with love,
Surmount all trials with grace,
Perform great things
By mastering small details.

Surely the world's big problems
Can be traced to simple causes,
Just as great events arise
From humble beginnings.

With this in mind the wise
Will do their utmost without pretense,
Working wonders with
The smallest means--
And this, despite those whose
Rash promises lack good faith,
And those too at ease
With important things,
Are too self-important
For the simple things.

Along The Way
The wise take all things
Equally to task,
And measure out their days
In peace.

Poem Sixty-Four

DARING TO KEEP THINGS SIMPLE

How easy things are
Maintained before they move,
Adjusted before they're set,
Foreseen before they arise,
All details attended to
While clear and distinct.
Better to solve problems
Before they appear and
Tend to things while order prevails.

For the stubbornest vine
Was once a sprout,
The tallest tower,
But a mound of earth,
The wildest goose chase
Began with a flutter.
To force the issue
Or make a fuss
Defeats your purpose.
When you grab or clutch at things
They tend to slip away.

So it's wisest to avoid
The meddlesome touch,
Or the selfish reach,
And keep things easily in hand.
The contrary fault is
To quit too soon.
Failing to follow through
Will surely spoil the day.

The sagely Way attends
The course of events
From start to finish and
Avoids the path to ruin.
Thus sages mind what matters,
Check desire's rush,
Avoid impossible schemes
And dreams of riches,
Shun the pedant's waste of words,
And recover what most people
Give up in mindless haste.

Attending to the natural flow of things,
The wise assume no risk
And incur no blame.
With nothing to venture
They have all life to gain.

Poem Sixty-Seven

THREE TREASURES: CARING, SHARING, OPENING

All the world says The Way of Life
Is a wonder without equal.
Perhaps its greatness lies in just
This being beyond compare.
If it ever had a peer
Its uniqueness would long ago
Have disappeared.

Speaking of matters of measure--
Behold three treasures which are
The stay and power of life:
      Loving care,
      Being fair,
      Being humble.
For to care extends the heart
And gives one courage to go on.
To be fair is to share the whole,
And so enlarge one's world.
To be humble leaves an open place
For others while saving room for growth.

But being brash without caring
Is simply reckless.
Being rich without sharing
Diminishes one's world.
Being first in line is
A lonely and third rate space indeed!

What need is there of death
If we live like this?
Kindness in life's contest

Is the best defense
And wins over all.
For heaven is an ever-present guide
To those who walk
The compassionate Way.

Poem Seventy-Six

PUTTING THE HIGH AND MIGHTY IN THEIR PLACE

The newly born
Are soft and supple,
While the dead grow
Quickly hard and rigid.
All things when young
Are tender as grass
And pliant as a sapling.
But deathly age finds them
Brittle and dry.

A weakness withered and stiff
Is the mark of all
Fellow-travelers of death.
But life's companions are
Gentle and yielding.
Old growth will soon give way;
The great and mighty lose their place.
Yet the way things are,
The soft and supple
Grow and flourish.

PART FOUR:

THE WAY OF THE WAY

Poem One

THE EXTRAORDINARY WAY

The Way things are
Is so extraordinary
No name or shape can give away
The secret of this Word
Behind all tongues.

Though of unnamed source,
The wordless chant calls all things forth--
Nature's tune recalled by creatures
As a Mother's song.
(Nurture is the Way)

To calm the waters of desire
Is to see one's way
Clear to the source.
Yet to ride the waves of passion
One may indeed behold
Life's endless shore.

As wonderfully as a road divides
And joins itself again,
The inward and outward path are one.
This mystery opens the gate
Of the world's wonders.

Poem Four

FULL AND DEEP, CALM AND CLEAR

The Way is a well unfathomed,
Fresh for every use.
In this overflowing spring
We find the ultimate resource
Replenishing all.

Its waters give us power to
    Dull life's daggers,
    Unfasten fetters,
    Tone down the glare,
    And temper the pace
    Of the scurrying world.
None can say whose creation it is,
This form that precedes all gods.

Poem Five

CENTERING WITHOUT BIAS

It is nature's Way
To be unbiased--
All things both
Sacred and profane.
The sage, unbiased, too,
Treats the world
Just the same.

For the cosmic span
Is like a bellows
Producing power
As it goes.
All talk retires quickly
Before this truth--
Inner balance holding sway.

Poem Six

DARK MOTHER OF THE WORLD

The springs of spirit flow forever
As creation's Mother is veiled in mist.
From the gateway of this
Feminine depth of things
All nature comes to birth--
A valley so vast,
A source so fresh,
No toil attends your work
If her labor becomes your task.

Poem Seven

HEAVEN IS, EARTH ABIDES

The constant sky
And the enduring earth
In selflessness hold
The secret of life's
Endlessness.

Just so, sages,
Displacing ego,
Denying self,
Find themselves
Exalted and immortal--
The pinnacle of
Selfless interest.

Poem Eleven

HOW NOTHING IS USEFUL

As a wheel's spokes
Join at the hub,
Voiding forces as they work,
Thus is a coach deployed.

As clay is shaped
Into vessels and
Hollowed for use,
Or windows and doors
Are cut out from a wall,
So by its not being at all,
A hole makes its best effect.

Such is the profit and use
Of being and non-being
Together at work.

Poem Fourteen

THE WILD GOOSE CHASE: A TALE OF THE WAY

What goes unnoticed,
Though we look,
Appears to be invisible.
What remains unheard,
Though we listen
In silent suspense,
Ever eludes us,
Untouched by reaching hands.

What's behind these probes
Is indeed unsearchable.
Yet whatever it is
That draws us beyond our grasp,
Merges in continuous creation.

The luminous face of things
Is veiled in mystery.
Yet its soul is clear and deep.
The tale of a place unspeakably vast
Where all things return
To nothingness--
A form that never appears--
An image without a shape.

A notion so mad and abstruse
Must still be faced,
Though its heart be missed;
Pursued, though we scarcely
Glimpse its trail.

Hold fast to the ageless Way
By attending what is
Present at hand.
Such is to know
The Primal Beginning,
The Tale of The Way.

Poem Twenty-One

WILD AND CALM AND SURE

True Power has only
One way to flow.
For the Way of nature
Is untamed yet so refined...
The very heart of wildness
Encompassing all.

The Core of Life--
So calm,
So dark,
So deep,
So pure--

No surer truth than this holds sway:
Unfathomable power pervading
All the myriad forms of things.

All ages unfailingly recall its name,
This witness of all beginnings.
How do I know about
Creation's genesis?
It's The Way things are!

Poem Twenty-Five

ALL CREATION COMES HOME TO DWELL WITH THE MOTHER

Behind creation's work there stands
A presence more and less than real,
Encompassing even chaos!
Vast and calm and changeless,
It abides and works its
Solitary Way unhindered--
A Cosmic Mother enfolding
The heavens and the earth
With infinite ease and care.

As her true name is beyond recall,
I simply say it is "The Way of Life."
Pushed to summon more expansive words,
Perhaps I'd recollect life's grand
And everlasting venture--
All things great and small
Going forth always to return
To the Mother.

As the Great Way extends itself
To embrace the heavens and the earth
And humankind, so, too,
Our sagely rulers dwell among
The Four Great Powers
In Creation's span.

People would do best to tend their lives
In accord with earthly devotion.
For the nurturing earth by nature
Follows the clear and high Celestial Road.
And in its vast and silent turning

The sky's great arc attends
Life's radiant Power
Which leads The Way.
All creation follows
Quite naturally.

Poem Forty

YIELD AND RETURN TO THE WAY

Recovering The Path
Is the way things work--
Opening up and yielding
Is how they come home by it.

All creatures great and small
Arise from the sphere
Of concrete being.
And this luminous orb of life
Springs forth out of nothing
But The Way.

Poem Forty-One

TRUE POWER IS A FREE AND PERFECT BLESSING

Great sages on their Way
Attend to the Word
Behind all tongues
And follow through accordingly.
Average seekers listen
To the words along their Path
But waver in heeding it.
Pedantic scholars hear
About The Way of Life,
But merely scoff or mock.

If, to such fools,
It were not laughable,
It wouldn't be authentic anyway!
Ancient wisdom tells us
The Way of Light appears obscure,
The Upward Path suggests retreat,
The Middle Road seems harsh and narrow.

Likewise, spirit at the peak
Of fitness appears degraded,
And purity of heart lacks outward grace;
The great of soul seem stingy,
The resolute somehow suspicious,
The truly honest, merely fake.

Nevertheless, those of boundless spirit
Have nothing to hide, yet
Their greatest talents are never spent,
Their best songs remain unsung,
Their fairest form is unimagined.

For the true Way of Life,
Hidden beyond any glib recall,
Brings deliverance and fulfillment
As a matter of course.

Poem Forty-Five

CALM AND CLEAR, PURE AND SIMPLE

The most perfect can seem deficient,
Yet it never fails to function.
The most complete may have
An empty look about it,
But its use is inexhaustible.
The most exact at times
Can seem somehow wrong,
The greatest skill may
Come off as clumsy,
And the fairest words
Appear to fumble.

So in the same strange way
Movement overcomes cold,
And stillness conquers heat.
Getting clear and working through
These things one finds
The world's true measure.

Poem Forty-Seven

BEHOLD THE CELESTIAL WAY

No need to pass your garden gate
To know the world,
Nor peer through windows
To see the celestial road.
The more you go out of your way
To travel, the less you see
Of essential living.

The sagely Way
Avoids the round about,
And figures it out--
Divines the truth
Without defining terms,
And so completes the task at hand
With never a flinch or fuss.

Poem Fifty-One

THE WAY OF GENESIS IS THE SECRET OF ALL POWER

All creation springs from The Way
Amid a nurturing Power
As the concrete world of things
Provides some manner of form,
And circumstance completes
Their final shape.

All creatures stand in awe of The Way
And respect the Power of its workings--
Not from duty, but quite naturally.
Thus, The Way gives life
As its sure and subtle strength
Works to nurse and raise all things,
Support and discipline them,
Protect and perfect them
As they ripen and go their way.

This is how one can
Bring forth life without possession--
Create but not claim,
Raise but not impose.
It is the deep and open secret
Of life's true power.

Poem Fifty-Two

YIELD AND COMING HOME ARE HABITS OF THE EXTRAORDINARY

In the beginning
The Way of Life
Gives birth to the world
As a Mother.
In communion with the Mother
We sense the community of her children.
In truly knowing her children
Our care returns to the Mother.
In this way we can
Face death without risk or fear.

Master the gates of passion,
Guard the doors perception,
And be untroubled for
The measure of your days.
But let loose your tongue,
Meddle in worldly matters,
And you are beyond hope.

Just as a sense of scale
Makes things clear and true,
So does the yielding Way
Gain in strength.
A torch may light the path,
But only insight comes home
Without losing the way.
Such are the habits of
The extraordinary.

Poem Seventy

SIMPLE WORDS, EASY TASKS

The language of The Way
Is so simple to grasp,
The Path quite easy to follow.
Yet the world is unable to see it
Or take it to task.

Inexorably,
These sayings have a source,
The deeds before them a master
Unknown to people
Even as I am unknown.

Rare indeed are those
Who share the vision
And find me worthy.
Yet under the sagely sackcloth
Hides the jade of truth.

Poem Seventy-One

KNOWING ONE'S IGNORANCE IS THE HEIGHT OF WISDOM

On the high road of Truth
Are those who know
How little they know.
But those who pretend to know
Find only the misery born
Of Ignorance.

So sages,
Clearly aware
Of delusion's disease,
Keep fit in their wisdom and
Are free to go on their Way.

JOTTINGS ON THE WAY TO PEACE

An Introduction And Thematic Commentary On

LAO TZU'S TAO TEH CHING

Tracking down quotations: Poems cited are followed by numbers in parentheses. Roman numerals refer to one of the four-part collection of themes (Page 4). The second number is the poem number. The third number is the stanza. Find the poem number in the Index on Page 179 to take you to the poem in this edition.

Among the numerous translations in traditional format one can find many useful and scholarly introductions to Lao Tzu and the book commonly ascribed to him, the *Tao Teh Ching*. The present translation and rearrangement of Lao Tzu's poems is designed to help a troubled world and confused souls find the road to peace. Hence, the focus of this Introduction is on exploring the dimensions and dynamics of a non-aggressive mode of power for our species living on the earth. The chapter follows a path of reflection on a dozen or so Taoist qualities illustrated through the Chinese symbol-characters that represent them. By meditating on the concrete image and its complex of association we may then comprehend each facet of the Way of Peace and also appreciate the interconnections among them.

The reflection on the symbol moves toward an intuitive awareness of the essential qualities of the Way. This mediation of meaning through symbols is important to Lao Tzu's approach. He cautions us at the outset of his attempt at communicating profound but ultimately inexpressible truths about the Way Things Are: It is "so extraordinary/ No name or shape gives voice/ To this Word behind all tongues." (IV, I, I) The poet-sage, certain that the Ultimate is ungraspable directly in image or concept, is equally confident that words and symbols can nonetheless point us in the approximate direction, and perhaps even give us the impetus to move. Something as subtle and pervasive, concrete and abstract, important and elusive as the essential energy of life requires a language beyond the ordinary range of clear and distinct philosophic terms. Such "irrational" meanings and realities are not vague and imprecise. It is simply that ordinary rational discourse is not the right tool for comprehending this dimension of things. But rather than "coming down" to the level of symbolic and poetic language, one, in fact, expands to a vocabulary of living, feeling, and acting in a much wider horizon of application and with a profounder reach of soul.

The assumption is that there is a primal oneness, a suchness at once beyond and within all things. Our concepts and images and senses reach out straining and clutching. But a deeper sense tells us:

> What's behind these probes
> Is indeed unsearchable.
> Yet whatever it is
> That draws us beyond
> Our grasp merges in
> One creation.
> The luminous face of things
> Is veiled in mystery
> Yet its soul is clear and deep.
> It is the tale of a place
> Unspeakably vast
> Where all things
> Return to nothingness—

A form that never appears—
An image without a shape.
A notion so mad and abstruse
Must still be faced,
Though its heart be missed;
Pursued, though we scarcely
Glimpse its trail. (IV, 14, 2-4)

So it is with high seriousness and subtle humor that Lao Tzu opens his book by telling us that the Way is beyond words, and then goes on to write eighty-one poems! In effect he has provided us with a working dictionary of signs in the hieroglyphics of life, a guidebook on recovering the path, a collection of natural and homely metaphors to meditate on and mediate the confusing clarities of ordinary learning and the ambiguities of common living.

Our task at this point is to approach the Extraordinary Way of Peace not by grasping or penetrating concepts, but by opening up to and receiving the vital truth about power and peace as it naturally comes through us. The sagely way of knowing is yin rather than yang. The method of yin is not passive, but a dynamic nurturing and receptiveness. This yin quality we will explore further in this Introduction, especially around the symbol of Mother. As we take each symbol-character in turn, we will consider its etymology, its image, and its concrete connotations. We will then move into the larger sphere of its metaphorical expressions of ethical, spiritual, and metaphysical meaning.

It is important to keep in mind that these symbols are suggestions—or better, evocations. They are a "calling forth" of an intuition of essential forms or characters of things. The interpretive frame of reference will be to comprehend how the dynamics of peace are not merely an ideal or hope, but a force and dimension inherent in the very essence of things as they really are. Lao Tzu's vision and invitation are that peace is the natural way of life. Our challenge is to recover the deeper source of it and raise ourselves to the higher ground of shared and fulfilled living together in a common and wondrous creation. Let us look, then, through the symbols touching the basic principles of life itself. The researches and reflections along the Way are intended as starting points for the reader's own personal appropriation of the deeper motive interests of spirit and to provide a springboard for action.

I. THE SYMBOL OF TAO OR THE WAY THINGS ARE

Lao Tzu's famous and enigmatic TAO or Way is, in fact, a common Chinese word consisting of a two-part image, the left and lower figure being a word root or radical whose group of associated characters all denote process, change, motion, action. It literally depicts the feet of a person walking. The upper part is the head of a chieftain or perhaps of an antlered animal, i.e. one who leads or is a chief.

The common meanings of the character are road, path, method, reason, word, speech, doctrine. The Greek equivalent would be LOGOS. At this level the word TAO connotes the ultimate reality beyond yet somehow within its concrete manifestations. Now if we survey this family of meanings, we get a definite and suggestive answer to the metaphysical question: what is there? what is reality? Contained in the TAO symbol is a descriptive clue to a fundamental intuition of Reality as One, encompassing, everlasting, measureless field of change—innumerable things coming to be and passing away. There are objects and events, and there is order, both local and cosmic. But these forms and concrete things are principles or patterns or process; the universe goes on endlessly, albeit in varied rhythms. Form is not more or less real than feeling; ideals not more or less real than things; eternity not more or less real than concrete events. They are in each case two sides of the same reality, each incomplete and meaningless apart from the other. If this all seems a bit abstract, our sage summons us to recover the sense of existence opening from wonder to wonder as an infinite series of windows and gates.

Lao Tzu's emphasis on provoking a sense for the nature of things is on the unity within the variety, centeredness in the vortex, tranquility in the commotion, harmony blending the discord, and community flowering from the sharing of individuals. The Way is not the mere terminus of mystical contemplation or ascetic practice or intellectual exercise. It is simply the higher exponent, the deeper ground and wider frame of ordinary living. That is why I have often translated CHANG TAO or Eternal Way as the Extra-Ordinary Way: awareness of the Eternal is an uncommon seeing and embracing of the Way Things Are in their amazing wholeness and suchness:

> The Way Things Are
> Is so extraordinary...
> To calm the waters of desire
> Is to see life clear to the source;
> Yet to ride love's tide one may
> Indeed behold life's endless shore.
> As wonderfully as a road divides
> And joins itself again.
> The inward and outward path are one.
> This mystery opens the gate
> Of spirit's depth. (IV, 1, 1,3,4)

If we recall the root meaning of the pictogram-character for TAO, we find ourselves enjoined to follow the path of the widest and highest of beings, the entire community of life itself. Every common thing is transfigured in the light of the vast organism of creation. The smallest creatures in their nooks and crannies are not irrelevant details or forgotten diversions in the grand revolution and evolution of the universe. Plato called the ultimate Good (TAO) the perfect and encompassing living creature. Spinoza speaks of knowing and acting in the form and light of eternity. And Hindu sages tell us even more personally and radically that we are the ultimate Being, the deepest Self of the universe, and so is every other being an extension and reflection of the One. It is the principle and fact of each individual's identity with the Way and its subtle Power. It also entails our affinity and bond with each creature. The invitation and imperative is to know it and act accordingly.

Now what does this mean in the nitty gritty demands of everyday living and working and playing? It is a matter of taking the standpoint of the other beings in your life and indeed the whole sphere of life itself as your self and task. Jesus put it quite clearly and directly: You love God with all that you are, knowing that your neighbor and your self are part of the same Divine Life. We share one life as sisters and brothers of an eternal parent:

> Only those who care
> For the world
> As their widest self
> May live and hold
> The world in trust. (III, I3, 3)

This knowledge of who we really are in relation to each other and the comprehensive sphere of life is not primarily an intellectual act. It is an empowering realization that liberates and energizes the individual. When you become aware of the truth about the Way of Life as a community you cultivate it in daily affairs. It is an insight that quickens the world around us and spreads its influence far beyond our immediate horizon:

> Never cease to cultivate
> The true Way of Life.

Putting its powers to the test
Is what brings out your truth.
Its power nurtured in the family
Yields the warmth and joy
Of abundant life.
Its power working in community
Makes way for growth more lasting
And effective in a wider sphere.
Its power fostered in the nation
Sustains the golden horn of plenty.
Its power spread throughout the world
Is boundless resource gracing every table. (III, 54, 1-3)

History testifies to the fact that great cultural figures in art, religion, philosophy, science, and statecraft sometimes seem to touch deeper resources of being and truth and so manifest a profound spiritual force. It is often characterized by a magnetic pull among intimates and other contemporaries, while generating radiant waves of transforming power on subsequent epochs. Nevertheless, though we point to these dynamic personal centers of creativity, Lao Tzu reminds us, as many poets, saints, and sages do, that they are simply agents or vessels of the natural Way of things. The Taoist sage suggests that whatever good we do is only an "unlocking of life's creative power." (II, 10, 4) Genius is a matter of finding it "in the power of your earthbound soul/ To remain whole and not be scattered." (II, 10, 1) If credit be given at all, it is not to the ego but to the Way itself. For "as heaven unveils the given forms of things," the inner imperative and challenge is to "devoutly keep the vision clear, encompassing all/ Avoiding vain pretense and blind misuse." (II, 10, 3)

In the final count Lao Tzu would have us refrain from dwelling too much on the genius of others and risk losing the Way ourselves. So the wise take momentous things with seriousness and life's raging furies with wit and grace. In this way,

> Sages travel on and on
> Bearing their burdens lightly,
> Taking dazzling vistas
> In their stride. (I, 26, 2)
> Yet the smallest wonders
> On the sage's path
> Work with undiminished effect. (III, 35, 3)

So there is no need for us to compare ourselves with the world's worthies. The springs of spirit flow wide and deep and channel themselves in the most unexpected and out of the way places. Indeed, if you are concerned with "going in style", in the most transcendental sense of the term,

> Behold the extraordinary way
> Life transforms itself!
> Go forth before the world's wonders
> Untouched, contented,
> At ease in the extravagance
> Of Peace. (III, 35, 1)

II. THE SYMBOL MU: NATURE AS MOTHER, THE WAY OF NURTURE

Lao Tzu gives us the richest clue to finding and following the Extraordinary Way of Life by gathering his symbols and reflections around homely metaphors rather than leaving us stranded or lost in the elusive notion of a path—or merely the TAO, as some English translators dodge their task. Mystery, wonder, and a touch of madness are one thing in the ample world of the Way. But mystification and obscurity are the pedants' tricks for fooling mostly themselves. Even on the intellectual plane concepts like "encompassing unity," "universality," "transcendence," etc., boggle the mind. But the sage who left us with these eighty-one poems or jottings on the Way definitely prefers to communicate insight into the inexpressible through the concrete images of water, wood, wind—and perhaps his favorite name for the Way as Mother.

In its modern form the word MU, meaning mother or female, is a stylized form streamlined for writing the older cursive pictogram of a woman drawn with prominent breasts. If the current character is turned on its side and the ancient circular script is recalled, the image is obvious. By association and extension the word is appropriated for a whole family of metaphoric uses: earth, source or resource, productivity, a dam, a local ruler.

In Lao Tzu's book Mother is the primary symbol for the Way Things Are. In the opening poem he reminds us that the ultimate reality and ground of things is beyond definition or concept. Nevertheless, he says if we would call up its essential quality in something nameable, the nurturing way of Mother Nature might come close:

Though of unnamed source,

The wordless chant calls all things forth—
Nature's tune recalled by creatures
As a Mother's song,
Nurture holding sway. (IV, 1, 2)

As the encompassing cosmic as well as local field of energy, the Way of Creation is nature as nurture. Matter, mater (Latin), or mother, the nourisher, provider, sustainer. Drawing on the everyday meanings of maternal care as near at hand, Lao Tzu suggests that the Way is not some far-off Transcendent Other or abstract principle, or supernatural force. It is a subtle and immediate power effective in the local situations of life:

All creation springs from the Way
Amid a nurturing power
As the concrete world of things
Provides some manner of form,
And circumstance completes
Their final shape. (IV, 51, 1)

We often fail to notice or appreciate the Mother's workings, not because they are abstruse and vague, but because they are constant, untiring, and pervasive. Inevitably by our ignorance and ingratitude we are brought up short in her presence manifest in the wonderfully complex schemes of recurrence that are her ways and means:

All creatures stand in awe of the Way
And respect the power of its workings,
Not from duty, but quite naturally.
Thus, the Way gives life
As its sure and subtle strength

Works to nurse and raise all things,
Support and discipline them,
Protect and perfect them
As they ripen and go their way. (IV, 51, 2)

Thus, the Taoist sage now brings the essence of the Way as Mother even closer to us, namely to our character and part in the community of things. He urges us not merely to depend on nature's providential resourcefulness, but to assist in her beautiful enterprise and take on her qualities in our own tasks. The invitation and urging is to become as parent, as mother of creation in your particular world:

This is how one can
Bring forth life without possession,
Create but not claim,
Raise but not impose.
It is the deep and open secret
Of life's true power. (IV, 51, 3)

In one of his most ethically profound passages Lao Tzu illuminates the wonderful freedom that belongs to a loving and giving spirit—one that combines the yang energy of firmness and initiative, the yin power of loving care, and the innocence and simplicity of the very young child, offspring of yin and yang:

To face the adventure of your life
With creative courage
Yet maintain a spirit
Of humble nurture,
Simply sustain the world

In its course as if
You were its valley.
Conduct the living stream
This natural way and so
Recover that extraordinary
Freshness and fitness of a child. (II, 28, I)

Returning once again to the wider horizon of the Mother image, the sage would have us recover some of the cosmic mystery of this natural and unending love. In a very terse and beautiful poem jotted down in just twenty-five characters, the poet-mystic invites us to cast wide the net of our metaphysical imagination:

DARK MOTHER OF THE WORLD

The springs of spirit flow forever
As creation's mother is veiled in mist.
From the gateway of this
Feminine depth of things
All nature comes to birth.
A fertile womb so vast
And lasting
No toil attends her task. (IV, 6)

In a similar frame and reach of mind, though more philosophically wordy and reflective, Lao Tzu reverses the conceptual leap of his first poem (IV, I, I-2) where he moved from the ineffable and nameless Way to the more accessible calling of the Mother. The first of the following stanzas in Poem Twenty-five invokes the dark presence of the Cosmic Yin: the vast sea of Being. In the second stanza we encounter a somewhat rare moment of self-consciousness in the sage—an awareness and humble amazement at discovery. It is the not quite expected and lucky find in the search for means to convey this Word behind all tongues: (IV, 1,1)

> Underlying all creation's work
> There stands a presence
> More than real
> Encompassing even chaos.
> Vast and calm and changeless
> It abides and works its
> Solitary Way unhindered—
> A Cosmic Mother enfolding
> The heavens and the earth
> With infinite care.
>
> As her true name
> Is beyond recall,
> I simply say it is
> "The Way of Life."
> Pushed to summon more expressive words,
> Perhaps I'd recollect
> Life's grand and everlasting venture—
> All things great and small
> Going forth only to return
> To the Mother. (IV, 25, 1,2)

And as if to answer boldly the inevitable wonder of plain folk, or the skepticism of the learned, our philosopher on his Way leaves humility behind:

> The Core of Life—
> So calm, so dark, so deep, so pure—
> No higher truth than this holds sway:
> Unfathomable power pervading
> All the myriad forms of things.
> All ages unfailingly recall its name
> This witness of all beginnings.
> How do I know about creation's genesis?
> It's the Way things are! (IV, 21, 2,3)

If all this indeed be so, that "True power has only one Way to flow," (Ibid, st. I) in the Mothering nature of things, then the power of yin is essential to creating, recovering, and keeping peace in the natural community of life. With wonderful simplicity of image and directness of expression Lao Tzu combines the vastness and depth of the Cosmic Mother with the relevance of her power and presence to our personal lives:

> In the beginning
> The Way of Life
> Gives birth to the world
> As a mother,
> In communion with the mother
> We sense the community of her children.
> In truly knowing her children
> Our care returns to the mother.
> In this way we can
> Face death without risk or fear. (IV, 52, I)

Both practically and spiritually our lives will attain a higher level of success and bring us happiness and peace if we allow a sense of scale to light our path and ease our burden. For if the Way Things Are is such that power is shared and distributed, then it is false as well as foolish to grab power to oneself. Indeed, the local fact and cosmic truth bear it out that the yielding way of yin is what truly gains in strength.

As we saw in meditating on the TAO, the Way, what we need to do is identify with the whole of things and each of its parts; so the Way of Life as a Mother's nurturing power can become the calling of each of us. It centers on being more fully what you are in giving and sharing with others. In a single concise poem Lao Tzu draws on the image of our parents in the natural sphere, earth and sky, yin and yang, to provide models for peaceful balance in the challenging art of living:

HEAVEN IS, EARTH ABIDES

The constant sky
And the enduring earth
In selflessness hold
The secret of life's endlessness.
Just so, sages,
Displacing ego,
Denying self,
Find themselves
Exalted and immortal—
The pinnacle of
Selfless interest. (IV, 7, 1,2)

And finally, our Taoist mentor extends and applies to the political sphere the natural norm of power as Mother. It is a matter of conservation, distribution, and balance; an ode to metaphysical Motherhood:

NATURE'S POWER: THE HABIT OF RESOURCEFULNESS

When it comes to ruling people
And tending the Celestial Way
Nothing surpasses conserving
Force and resource.
Such sparing ways simply mean
Having foresight to gather and store
Life's power through which
All things are possible.
Only one in whom the power of
Goodness is natural,
Boundless, and irresistible,
Is truly fit to rule the realm.
When nature's balance
Is the mother of a people,
They endure.
The tree of community
Deeply planted,
Growing strong,
Will stand forever
In the light of the Way. (II, 59)

III. THE NATURE OF TEH OR THE FINER WAYS AND MEANS OF LIFE'S FLOW OF ENERGY

The notion of TEH is a keystone in Lao Tzu's insight into the dynamics of living. It is so important, in fact, that it stands beside TAO, the Way, in the title of his book: TAO TEH CHING. Indeed the work has long been divided into two parts: The Book of the Way, poems 1-37, and The Book of Moral Power, poems 38-81. Very roughly grouped, the first part is more general and metaphysical; the second part, more concrete and ethical. Of course, many down-to earth expressions are found in the former division and more abstruse reflections in the latter. At any rate, the character-symbol TEH presents perhaps more complexity and difficulty for the translator than any of the other major notions in our introduction.

As a beginning and intermediate worker in a number of languages I cannot quite justify the defensive dodge of many translators in the face of the challenge of bridging the gap between languages. It is often claimed that a particular word cannot be rendered directly into English. What is meant is that no single word equivalent is adequate to the original. Certainly Robert Frost is right in saying that tone and poetry are "what get lost in translation." But finery of style aside, I would insist that essential meaning and universal truth can be transplanted from one linguistic soil to another, though it takes radical pruning and site preparation. In short, a phrase or even a sentence may be required to transpose the root meaning of the first tongue. The Chinese symbol for TEH is our prime and present example.

If we take it back to its basic radical or stems we find the primary image on the left a common combining form meaning "to step, walk, go, proceed," carrying with it the connotation of measured or regulated pace. The pictograph on the right from top to bottom denotes a cross for "ten", a divided box for "eye," a line below the box contracted from a 90 degree angle meaning "straight, true, right, correct;" and below that the stylized markings abbreviated from the image of a heart with its lobes. Taken together this means literally: what ten eyes, or the attentively observing community, agrees is right, taken seriously, authentically, in purity of heart. What the right hand image thus suggests is that singleness of purpose goes with the impassioned clarity of the upright heart. Righteousness is a moral consensus bespeaking universal intent as well as personal commitment. When conjoined with the forthright and measured step indicated on the left side of the character, the word carries with it the impetus and resolve to action, to concrete realization.

In its linguistic integrity TEH is a cluster of symbols uniting three dimensions of moral virtue: the reflective-intuitive, the affective-existential, and the active or practical. Another division might be the objective, subjective, and projective. Put more directly and less technically, it is the wholeness of the head, the heart, and the foot: getting together one's knowing, feeling, and doing.

One can see why various usages in the Chinese idiom combined with the diverse dispositions of the translators have brought out one or more of the complex connotations of the word TEH: virtue, goodness, discipline, character, excellence, benefit, accomplishment, flourishing, realization, power, energy. Witter Bynner's rendering of TEH as moral or spiritual "fitness" is a worthy and effective translation. Perhaps the existential quality of "authenticity," or Carlos Castaneda's personal power finding a "path with heart", also come close to this compact and important Chinese character that contains a complete moral philosophy.

As we look at this quality in the context of several of the poems, we should keep in mind a long tradition common to many eastern and western philosophies and religions. There are, of course, a number of distinct virtues and paths of conduct expressing diverse qualities. But moral excellence or spiritual fitness is basically a unitary power. Differences of detail, outward form, personal style, and special function are natural and inevitable just as eddies, ripples, and branching streams form one river, or waves, swells, and tides comprise one ocean. For one finds:

> True power in the Way
> Varied streams and rivers
> Flow toward one
> Great Sea. (II, 32, 5)

In truth all of the remaining symbols in this Introduction are forms and dimensions of virtue. Here we will consider some insights not directly developed later. At the end of this section I will also refer the reader to particular poems bearing on specific qualities.

At the beginning of this section on TEH, I referred to Part Two of Lao Tzu's work as The Book of Moral Power. A more specific title might be "The Book of Moral Fitness in Action." As befits the complexity of subject, this first poem is one of the longest in the entire book. Though the original manuscript gives no titles to the individual poems, I have assigned them thematic signatures or keynote expressions that suggest or introduce something of what each piece contains. Poem Thirty-eight, which opens Part Two, I have styled "On Losing the Way and Its Power". In this case the sage's task is to convey what true spiritual power is by showing what it is not. The poem continues by pointing out what people look like who have lost it in varying degrees or have realized only a part of it. Those who are truly centered and on the Path are unselfconscious, unbiased, uncontentious, unsuspicious, imperturbable, unimpressed by formality, force, flimflam, or the wheel of fortune. When we come to understand virtue in its fullness and refinement we will see how moral power is dynamic in the way that the Mother, the yin quality is powerful:

> Humble masters of the art of life,
> These uncontentious spirits
> Remain at peace with the world.
> The ancient saying,
> "Yield with the Way and perfect the day,"
> Is more than empty wind.
> For yielding is the Way
> To recover true wholeness.
>
> So the noble soul abides
> With important matters at hand
> And doesn't dwell on superficial things.
> The sage enjoys the blossom,
> But attends to the harvest. (Ill, 38, 6,5)

Contrary to later stereotypes and historical expressions, the original and true Taoist is not a romantic religious idealist. Because the sagely Way is not to proceed by force or enforcement. Any need or desire to advance is effected by yielding, entreating, withdrawing, or embracing rather than bracing for a fight. So the sage is not likely to be martyred. However, the unconcern with appearance and formality may lead to misunderstanding:

The Way of Light appears obscure;
The Upward Path suggests retreat;
The Middle Road seems harsh and narrow.
Likewise, spirit at the peak
Of fitness appears degraded,
And purity of heart
Lacks outward grace,
The great of soul seem stingy,
The resolute somehow suspicious,
The truly honest, merely blunt.

Nevertheless, those of boundless spirit
Have nothing to hide, yet
Their greatest talents are never spent,
Their best songs remain unsung,
Their fairest form is unimagined.
The true Way of life,
Hidden beyond any glib recall,
Brings deliverance and fulfillment
As a matter of course, (IV, 41, 2,3,4)

Certainly in the long run, and usually even in the short run, the spiritually fit and centered not only find peace inwardly but express and establish it outwardly. The meaning of moral virtue goes beyond integrity and self-containment toward an effective, subtle radiating influence:

Heaven's Way does not contend,
Yet carries the day;
Speaks no word,
But finds response;

Without commanding,
Draws all to hand;
Works out its plan
With infinite patience. (I, 73, 2)

The sagely way accepts
The short end and
Makes no claim on others.
The wise work with skill
On the task at hand.
The fool holds back
And makes demands.
Though they seek no favors
On the Sacred Way
Sages find the yoke is easy
And the burden light. (I, 79, 2,3)

From the wisdom of Lao Tzu perhaps the central insight into peace is that, like love and charity, its realization begins and ends at home. If one is at war with oneself in the inner field of conflict of confused desires, motives, and purposes, one is not likely to be an effective means to peace in the world nearby let alone far away. The task starts with a quiet mastery of the senses. Right action demands clear vision:

Behold the Extraordinary Way
Life transforms itself!
Go forth before the world's wonders
Untouched, contented,
At ease in the extravagance
Of peace.

For even the smallest wonders
On the sage's Path
Work with undiminished effect. (III, 35, 1,3)

Pacification is above all self-transformation, a vital transformation of one's whole mode of living. For the Taoist this is the meaning of the peace that passes all understanding:

HOW GOOD TRANSFORMS THE SELF

Prudence searches others
But wisdom finds the self.
Force may conquer others
Where goodness transfigures life.
Know the treasures of contentment;
Persevere and brace your step;
Being at home in all the world
You outlast the longest journey
Finding death is but
A wayside inn. (I, 33)

Living your life on the Way of Peace widens the circle of beauty shared on the near side of things, as it surely connects us with whatever is best on the nether side of eternity.

NOTE: For insight into more specific qualities and particular twists and turns on the Way to inner and outer peace, see Part Three of this book. I have collected these poems around individual "Counsel to the People."

IV. THE POWER OF NON-BEING OR VIRTUE AS KNOWING WHAT TO AVOID

In reflecting on the nuances of TEH, moral fitness, we came to understand personal power and the nature of action in terms of community, rightness or appropriateness to context, and changing the world by changing oneself. Similarly in considering the Way Things Are and its essential yin qualities as Mother we found nature to be a field of caring and sharing of resource. In this light, being an individual is inescapably bound up with the togetherness and variety of things in a common world.

Now since the full range of acting and sharing and loving is unbounded in effect as well as affect, the task of perfecting life in the Sagely Way takes on the character of infinity. By virtue of its seeming enormity as a challenge to moral action, such an impossible dream could overwhelm us with a sense of futility and impotence. With everything to do, what, then, can we do? Where should we begin? Lao Tzu's amazing answer approaches the infinitude of the world's work from the other side of eternity. Since the teeming whirl of living and changing things is already building up or spinning off its diverse modes of order and harmony, probably the best way to tend one's affairs is, effectively, to not act much at all. In doing nothing by simply attending to the world's wonders, the sage accomplishes everything that needs to be done. This puzzling, even shocking strain of passivity and negativity in Lao Tzu's ethic of the Way figures most prominently in both its theoretical and practical ramifications. Therefore, we will consider here six notions Lao Tzu uses to convey the Way as Void, or Non-Being, and the way to act through Non-Action, or WU WEI.

In exploring the character-symbol TAO we already encountered its ineffable nature as something beyond definition,

conceptualization, or even direct reference. This nameless quality is
WU MING. The WU pictogram is a common and ancient mark of
negation imaging horses' feet running away and disappearing into
the woods to convey the sense of vagueness or the indefinite. MING
depicts a box below denoting a mouth and a crescent moon above
for dusk; i.e. when people or animals need to call out who or what
they are in order to be identified. Hence, MING means "name," or
what something is called. The TAO is WU MING, unnameable,
since the ultimate oneness of life and the amazing suchness of each
and all particular things is beyond our poor powers to compare or
call up in mere words. Signs, terms, and concepts are useful tools
that make sense figuratively and literally. But the whole and the part
are a kaleidoscope endlessly turning; so individual entities and their
forms are fixed only as an eyeblink abstraction or suspended
moment. To the enlightened, ordinary perception is the dazzling
appearance, the moving shadow over the depths; the Whole and its
showing are what is ultimate and what gives the movie screen of life
its context and reality:

> What goes unnoticed
> Though we look,
> Appears to be invisible.
> What remains unheard,
> Though we listen
> In silent suspense,
> Ever eludes us,
> Untouched by
> Reaching hands. (IV, 14)

The sage is not telling us that the rich tapestry of the foreground of life is not at all real, but that we lose ourselves in detail and narrow context, the outward games of perception and appetite:

> As too many colors
> May trick the eye,
> Or too much noise
> Confuse the ear,
> Or too many flavors
> Can jade one's taste,
> And just as the race and the hunt
> Make the mind go mad,
> And straining for riches
> Gets in the way of peace,
> So sages select and attend
> The more inward than outward
> Side of things and finally
> Come to their senses. (III, 12)

It should become clear to us, then, that wisdom as MING, picturing the double light of the sun and the moon, is not to be confused with knowledge as learning. The latter mode of knowing, CHIH, associated with the concept of MING for naming, connotes something more tunnelled, pointed, channelled, perspectival. It is adequate and necessary for special functions but is transcended in the art of living by a higher and wider vision of things. In the phrase MING PU CHIH the second word is a common mark of negation. The pictogram CHIH shows a long box on the right for mouth and an arrow being thrown. Thus, the precision, directedness, and selectivity of science in its determinate knowledge is at once its virtue and its vice. Where precise technical knowledge apprehends and projects pre-given structures and assumptions, with predetermined conclusions, intuitive knowledge comprehends wider groupings and interconnections beyond technical discourse and ordinary language. Lao Tzu was not really anti-intellectual. Tradition has it that he was a scholar and librarian by profession:

> Tend your lessons daily
> And your ego gains.
> Attend the Way of Life
> And your ego daily lessens,
> 'Til such diminishing
> Returns your ego
> To a less imposing state,
> Freeing your self
> To accomplish everything
> With little to do. (II, 48, 1)

The practical dilemma to be avoided is the categorical fix intellectuals get themselves into, as well as the endless verbal disputes with others over terms of disagreement:

> The wise abide in silence
> The endless verbal play of others.
> They master the gates of passion
> And guard the doors of expression (II, 56, 1)
> Better to be ignorant and unconcerned
> With the stickler's fuss about
> "Like and dislike" or
> "Good and bad."
> Best to avoid the endless tangles over

What to fear and not to. (III, 20, 1)

Perhaps the greatest fault of science and learning can be a disregard for respecting the limits of their special powers and horizons. The image of **PU CHIH** suggests a critical check on the power and direction of one's language games, their biases and limitations. It is caution against dogmatism or exclusiveness; hitting the mark while aiming at pre-set targets; not questioning the ground, scope or horizon of one's assumptions:

> On the high road of Truth
> Are those who know
> How little they know.
> But those who pretend to know
> Find only the misery born
> Of Ignorance.
> So sages,
> Clearly aware
> Of delusions' disease,
> Keep fit in their wisdom and
> Are free to go on their Way. (IV, 71, 1-2)

And if the habit of ordinary seeing and knowing is narrow perception and discourse **(CHIH)**, the corresponding tendency of human feeling and affection is bias: favoring and selecting this over that. The wisdom of the Way seeks to get beyond desire and love as preferential. So the attribute of **PU JEN** is to be cultivated. JEN, of course, is one of the cornerstones of Confucian philosophy. JEN has been variously translated as love, compassion, benevolence, human-heartedness, lovingkindness. The symbol depicts a contraction for person, and the number two. It conveys the intersubjective bond of feeling, the community of spirit that joins people in virtue of their common humanity and their individuality.

The Taoist critique of the notion of JEN entails an attitude of skepticism and practical wariness regarding the inveterate tendency of human affections toward prejudice and exclusiveness. Confucianists are aware of this, too; but the Taoist sage stresses that a truly free and compassionate self reaches below, above, and beyond mere human-heartedness to a transcending love—one that is as all-embracing as nature, the Mother of all things:

> It is nature's Way
> To be unbiased—
> All things both
> Sacred and profane.
> The sage, unbiased, too,
> Treats the world
> Just the same. (IV, 5, 1)

The Mother of all, attuned as She is with the Way Things Are, sets the measure and tone for living beyond good and evil, embracing and appreciating each creature in the vast and varied field of creation. Whoever collected and edited the traditional set of Lao Tzu's eighty-one poems most wisely chose a complete and enlightened philosophy of value in one poem to be placed immediately following the metaphysical mystery of the first. I quote it here in its entirety because it is so clear and direct in showing how non-being, not fussing, not clutching, and not favoring are the real means to positive living:

THE INTERPLAY OF BEING AND ITS SHADOW

Unable to see the good and fair
For what they are,
People set fixed norms,
Confusing effect for inner worth,
And so proscribe all sorts of
"Bad and ugly" things which
May not really be so.
From failing inner vision
They miss the interplay of Existence and its
shadow—

How distress and ease
Are phases in one work;
That what's long or short on skill
Are measured by a common task;
Why the high and lowly
Take each other's place;
That tone and pitch
Unite in single sound;
And what stays behind
May really lead the Way.

Accordingly, the sage
Attends to tasks without a fuss,
Instructs without a sermon,
Affirms all things as they arise,
Nurtures each but shuns possession,
Works without demand or claim,
Succeeds but doesn't dwell on it.
By not relying or gloating
On past success, the sage abides

All things along the Way. (III, 2)

Thus Lao Tzu expresses with wonderful simplicity and profound wisdom how it is that **PU JEN** is not inhumane or indifferent, but rather a farseeing and wide-reaching compassion—a love pervaded by impartiality, objectivity, unrestricted interest, and an appreciation that radiates outward to each and all.

Still another notion that seems to begin in negation but ends in affirmation and successful living is the way of **WU YU**. As in **WU MING**, cited earlier, **WU** reads here for "not," or "non." The left hand part of the character is a mouth or opening in the hills; i.e. a valley or ravine. On the right is pictured a person breathing out or out of breath, exhausted. By extension and generalization it means to owe, to be deficient or in debt. Combined as a metaphor these two pictograms graphically mean that desire or passion are like water rushing down and depleting itself if unchecked or unchannelled. So **WU YU** as non-desire implies a dispassionate use of one's vital energy. It is so central to Lao Tzu's philosophy of life that it figures as a key notion in the opening poem of the entire work. After calling forth the extraordinariness of the Way Things Are as a nameless yet pervading presence, or Motherhood, the eternal fecundity and providence of nature, the sage suggests to us:

> To calm the waters of desire
> Is to see life clear to the source;
> Yet to ride love's tide one may
> Indeed behold life's endless shore.
>
> As wonderfully as a road divides
> And joins itself again,
> The inward and outward path are one.

This mystery opens the gate
Of spirit's depth. (IV, I, 2,3)

Life is an endless river or sea of energy, a universe of tides and waves and currents, a labyrinth of channels, streams, and backwaters. The task is to make one's way knowing the local as well as wider courses and conditions of things. Not much more than a refinement of common sense, the way of WU YU or dispassionateness avoids the insistence and resistance of the normal rush and push of desire.

Drawing from a fund of ancient proverbs, the poet-sage shows us the practice behind the theory:

Deliberate when wading winter streams,
Careful of surrounding dangers,
Reserved as a grateful guest,
Yielding as melting ice,
Simple and unassuming as uncarved wood,
Open and obliging as a mountain vale,
Obscure as turbid water.

Who can render pure and calm
Life's muddy torrent?
Or nurture growth
From a quiet center,
Moving mountains
In the simplest style?

Those who trust the Way, of course!
Unconcerned with fulfillment,
Sages never overfill their day

And flourish in gray old age
Making life's late season
More like spring. (III, 15, 2-4)

The consequences of allowing the many-headed beast of passion to go its narrow, headstrong way is outer conflict and inner discord, With desire gone awry the name of the game is War; but its everpresent and natural alternative is Peace:

There is no greater misdeed
Than misspent passion;
No greater misfortune
Than lasting discontent,
Or quiet desperation;
No greater evil
Than desire for selfish gain.

It's better to see how much
Life simply holds in store
And so be ever content
Along the tranquil Way. (I, 46, 2,3)

And where do we get the model for this wider economy of vital force? Nature itself sets the rhythm and pace overall:

All in all
Stillness is the norm.
The rudest winds
Are quite soon spent;
And torrential rains
Prevail at most a day.

Even nature,
When aroused, lets up.
So much the more
Should it be for
Humbler human powers. (I, 23, 1,2)

Thus, the sagely advice to rulers in a community, as well as all those who would see to the proper and effective mastery of themselves, is the recovery of the natural law of balance and harmony inherent in the Way Things Are:

When people's channels of desire
Rise up and rage,
One directs them through
The nameless simplicity of nature.
In plain truth
The simple Way of Life
Free from the clutch
Of unbridled passion,
Keeps calm and clear.
In nature peace prevails
In due course. (II, 37, 2-4)

This gathering of poems around the notion of WU YU shows us how the way of non-desire or dispassionateness is one of the crucial lessons to be learned through reflection on the Great Way of Life. It is similar to the Buddha's pivotal insight that undisciplined desire is the root of all suffering. The wisdom of Lao Tzu does not call for the elimination of desire, but a mastery of passion: forces to be directed and distributed for the diverse purposes and interests of living. And as a problem with a natural solution built into it, the clue to working it out has been suggested in the very word or character-symbol itself.

Closely related to **WU YU** is the concept of **PU YU**, or non-possessiveness. **PU**, the mark of negation, precedes a striking image of the moon in the lower half and a hand above seizing or clutching it. The common meaning of the character is to grab, to get, to have. It also can mean to attain, succeed, possess, and even to exist. Using the ocean metaphor to get his insight across, the poet compares the Way of the Mother and a just ruler to the universal tide of replenishing resource:

> This universal flood
> Sustains and nurtures
> All creation without fail.
> One marvels at the way
> This sea completes its task
> But takes no honors.
> With loving care it raises
> Every creature without
> A dominating hand.
> Because it transcends
> The narrower currents of desire,
> The ocean's power works simply
> And with the gentlest touch.
> All things rise and recede
> With life's ocean swell;
> Yet the great tide claims
> Nothing for itself. (II, 34, 1-4)

We found earlier in reflecting on the Way and the Mother that the key to living and caring is selflessness, identification with the others in one's world. So here we can see that the error and issue of possessiveness is blindness to the profound interconnectedness of all things. It is a restrictive and exclusive boundary of self limited to this body, this ego, this or that object owned or controlled:

> Which is your most kindred self:
> Your fame or your frame?
> What counts more in loss or gain:
> Your wealth or your health?
> In losing, which causes the greatest pain?

> Consider, then, these sayings:
> Love over-extended
> Is life soon expended.
> Over-full coffers
> Promise great losses.

> So one finds that
> The highest grace is
> To be content with less.
> The lowest risk is
> To know when to stop.
> This is the secret
> Of growth and endurance. (III, 44)

The challenge both on a personal level and in the design and direction of a social organism is to cultivate a community sense of sharing and appreciation. It is better to head off discontent and conflict and so eliminate the need of devices for control and the repair of damage that social disorder can engender:

Void of cunning means and ways,
Renouncing private gain,
The people are no longer prey
To thieves and other malcontents.
Yet all this falls short of true culture.
In genuine community
People stick to what's reliable:
Finding simple ways
Embracing honest means
Limiting personal claims
Checking passion's flow. (III, 1,2)

The Way of Life as PU YU, non-possessiveness, obviously illuminates not only the issue of material possession but also the pursuit and wielding of power. Those who strive for domination labor under a mistake. The delusion that more power is better is quite simply a misunderstanding of the Way Things Are at any and all levels. Power, life, being, having, doing, and all other aspects and dimensions of living, comprise a shared reality, a distributed complex of functions:

One sees how power-hungry souls
Obsessed with molding
The world to their will
Seldom succeed for long.
The world is a sacred vessel
To be handled with a light
And reverent touch.
Clutch its power
And it will elude you. (I, 29, 1)

Why then do those whose will
Commands ten thousand chariots
Become so slight of soul
That their realm
Slips out of hand
And confusion takes the reins? (I, 26, 3)

The greatest masters
Rule vast realms
As dispassionate servants;
While those whose unruly passion
Is to take the world by storm
Are unfit to serve even themselves. (II, 48, 2)

Abuse of power inevitably undoes itself, though it usually leaves a trail of suffering and confusion in its wake. The truth is that all power and all life is yours if you, motherlike, assume the world as your charge, attending to it caringly rather than battling with it and taking charge aggressively. We note again the passage earlier cited in considering the Way of Nature as Mother. It brings home in the most direct and concise fashion the ultimate meaning of power and possession:

This is how one can
Bring forth life without possession,
Create but not claim,
Raise but not impose.
It is the deep and open secret
Of life's true power. (IV, 51, 3)

To conclude this fourth section on the various dimensions of "The Power of Non-Being" we must now ponder the famous Taoist teaching of WU WEI or Non-Action. It will round out and hopefully bring into clearer focus our discussion of Lao Tzu's notions of the Way of Life as negating or inverting the conventional perspective on loving, getting, having, ruling, and acting.

In the phrase WU WEI, WU denotes as it did in WU YU, no, not, or non, a common mark of negation. The character WEI is a frequently used word for doing or making. It is represented by a pictogram of a monkey fiddling with its hands. The illuminating image and interpretation here is that much, perhaps most, action in the human sphere is an idle fidgeting, or a wary and nervous response to the surroundings. The consequent "action" is with uneasy stillness or confused commotion. The massive norm of human affairs is in effect much ado about nothing, i.e. very little that is truly creative and a great deal of ineffective bungling. Lao Tzu's insight suggests then that true action seems and is more like non-action than the labored operations, forced cooperations, kneejerk reflexes, or clockwork mechanisms that we call "action." In fact, whether the world is or appears to be a mean machine or a merry mess, for the most part it remains quite beyond our poor power to effect or deflect its overall momentum and direction. The sage recommends that we not give up in despair or distraction. Staying cool and centered and not adding to the commotion or the problem is the first task:

> One finds advantage
> In making no fuss,
> And getting the point across
> By keeping still.
> How few, in the busy-ness

Of the world,
Profit by this insight! (I, 43, 2)

A sense of scale and a sense of humor are two effective tools to overcoming the frantic sense of "What to do, what to do?" The trick is not to be overwhelmed by the enormity of the world's weight, or become befuddled by its complexity, or waylaid by its attractions and diversions, or daunted by obstacles on the way:

> The Sagely Way
> Avoids the round about,
> And figures it out—
> Divines the truth
> Without defining terms,
> And so completes the task at hand
> With never a flinch or fuss. (IV, 47, 2)

The liberating power of WU WEI, acting without fussing or flinching, is not the delusion that one can do anything. It is rather the attitude that the world around you can do its thing, finding you in the path of least resistance free to accomplish your small part in the creativity of the world. The greatest and truest freedom is to assist the world on its path rather than insist on your own way. Creation is a collective enterprise—and so is freedom. Accepting the chances, changes, and necessities in your life, working with the small and subtle parameters of choice, you are able to "accomplish everything with little to do." (II, 48, 1)

> As momentous things
> May proceed with grace,
> And life's furious pace

May flurry about
Like a winter's snow,
So sages travel on and on
Bearing their burdens lightly,
Taking dazzling vistas
In their stride. (I, 26, 1,2)

One cannot deny that Lao Tzu's Wisdom of the Way presents us with not always easily grasped notions, inevitable practical difficulties, and perhaps ultimate mysteries beyond our reach. Nevertheless, it is this writer's conviction that Lao Tzu's main challenge and inspiration is for us to learn how easy it is to open up to the Way creation works and plays through us:

SIMPLE WORDS, EASY TASKS

The language of the Way
Is so simple to grasp,
The Path quite easy to follow.
Yet the world is unable to see it
Or take it to task.
Inexorably
These sayings have a source,
The deeds before them a master
Unknown to people
Even as I am unknown.
Rare indeed are those
Who share the vision
And find me worthy.
Yet under the sagely sackcloth
Hides the jade of truth. (IV, 70)

The simplicity and directness of the Way of WU WEI, or a no fuss, no bother mode of living, is encapsulated in a practical philosophy of Action as Non-Action found in Poems Sixty-three and Sixty-four. The inner and outer moral imperative is this: Touch the deepest springs and scout the widest range of action, and your walk will be a Way of Peace:

DOING WONDERS WITH EASE

Act without fuss
Serve without effort
Savor without excess
Exalt the lowly
Provide for the needy
Respond to hate with love
Surmount all trials with grace
Perform great things
By mastering small details.

Surely the world's big problems
Can be traced to simple causes,
Just as great events arise
From humble beginnings.

With this in mind the wise
Will do their utmost without pretense,
Working wonders with
The smallest means—
And this, despite those whose
Rash promises lack good faith,

And those too at ease with important things,
And too self-important
For simple things.

Along the Way
The wise take all things
Equally to task,
And measure out their days
In peace. (III, 63)

DARING TO KEEP THINGS SIMPLE

How easy things are
Maintained before they move,
Adjusted before they arise,
All details attended to
While clear and distinct.
Better to solve problems
Before they appear and
Tend to things while order prevails.

For the stubbornest vine
Was once a sprout,
The tallest tower,
But a mound of earth,
The wildest goose chase
Began with a flutter.
To force the issue
Or make a fuss
Defeats your purpose.

When you grab or clutch at things
They tend to slip away.

So it's wisest to avoid
The meddlesome touch,
Or the selfish reach,
And keep things easily in hand.
The contrary fault is
To quit too soon;
Failing to follow through
Will surely spoil the day.

The sagely Way attends
The course of events
From start to finish and
Avoids the path to ruin.
Thus sages mind what matters,
Check desire's rush,
Avoid impossible schemes
And dreams of riches,
Shun the pedant's waste of words,
And recover what most people
Give up in haste.

Attending to the natural flow of things,
The wise assume no risk
And incur no blame.
With nothing to venture
They have all life to gain. (III, 64)

V. THE THREE TREASURES: GOODNESS IN A NUTSHELL

I have heard it said in philosophical and theological circles that Lao Tzu's thought is mystical, irrational, poetic, intuitionist, unsystematic, and as such unsuitable as a consistent and viable ethical norm. It is hoped that through the course of these introductory studies the above stereotypes and misreadings will be shown to be patently absurd and untrue. The serious and attentive reader who has come this far in reflecting on Lao Tzu's symbols surely has come to appreciate the metaphysical grounding, existential authenticity, and practical cogency of these profound expressions on the Way. In working with the character-symbols of TAO and MU we explored the wide and deep metaphysical horizon of all things: the Way as nurture, or the concrete sphere of Nature as a region of objective support for creative schemes of recurrent forms and experiences. Then we pondered the notion of TEH as the nitty gritty working out of these patterns in local situations and taken to heart. Following this we proceeded to clarify and refine how the Way creatively functions through us and for us in a manner that is subtle and only apparently negative in comparison with the conventional aggressive approach to power and success.

Lao Tzu, as if to recover his own call to simplicity, gives us his ethical system in short form. Poem Sixty-seven accomplishes in a single stroke a concise and complete ethical imperative, a three-fold principle of the inner urge and outer workings of the Good. Thus the sage would show us that human beings, like the Cosmic Mother, possess natural and positive power for creative and harmonious living. And these forces for good are at once an immanent dynamic principle and a task to fulfill. The Three Treasures or measures of the Good Will as a means to the good life are: Love, Justice, and

Humility. Or put in more dynamic terms: caring, sharing, and opening. It is best not to fix on one single English equivalent for these qualities. We shall now range among their rich nuances and their ungetoverable power as prerequisites for living and doing well on the Way.

Lao Tzu's choice of the character PAO for treasures, values, or goods is a reminder to us that ultimate values are not intellectual abstractions or remote ends put off 'til retirement, or a Sabbath day, or the next three-week vacation. The pictogram describes gems, pottery, and money in a house. Things of great worth, even eternal import, are part of our dwelling place. As such they should function as part of the very rhythm and pace of our lives. When we consider what might constitute the three most basic values in the ultimate concerns of daily existence, the sage draws our reflection toward a more radical possibility: that these Three Treasures of our path among the goods around us may in fact be corollaries or dimensions of the Way itself: the standard and ground of all value beyond good and evil.

> Perhaps its greatness
> Lies in just this being
> Beyond compare.
> Speaking of matters of measure-
> Behold Three Treasures which are
> The stay and power of life:
> Loving care,
> Being fair,
> Being humble. (III, 67, 1,2)

In this translation I have pointed to the empowering and staying quality of these Three Goods, even though the original and most translations say "hold and protect," I have shifted the referent and direction of benefit to reinforce the insight that Lao Tzu brings home to us at the conclusion of the poem. We don't keep these standards out of an extrinsic sense of duty, or for some other reward or practical benefit, though these often will follow. We take the Way of love and fairness and openness because they are the Good Life itself, the fullness and perfection of living, the dynamic adventure of a community at peace in its creative enterprises. Every specific good is grounded and measured by this encompassing process toward the Good in the shared world.

Though the notion of love is cited first in the poem, it will be taken up last, as it is the most treasured of the Three Goods. It is their pivot and consummation. We move then to consider the second value, justness or fairness. The character pictogram CHIEN contains within it the essence of social reality, showing how its inner dynamic structure is grounded in the ambience of practical tasks. The left hand root is JEN for person as individual human being. The right hand configuration depicts at the top the roof of a house and a line under it conveying the idea of joining together or assembling under one roof. Below this line are two mouths and two persons. The whole image yields the idea of people talking or consulting and then coming to an agreement. The complex radical on the right hence means "whole, all, unanimity, consensus, or prevailing opinion." When the two-stroke figure is added, it carries the notion of thrift, economy, temperateness.

The practical wisdom contained in this Chinese word CHIEN conforms with Plato's analysis of the classic Greek virtue of Temperance and Justice as functional principles of social organization. As Justice is the timely and natural realization of each person's ability and task in the community, it corresponds to the principle of individuation in the left half of the Chinese character.

Temperance, or the function of self-rule in the social order, is the agreement of each person or operation as to who or what should govern them. Temperance, then, is a consensus regarding division of labor and power structure. This parallels the household meeting and conferring as denoted in the pictograph. Plato and Lao Tzu and the word-symbol itself show us that Justice and Temperance are distributive virtues operating through the relations between persons or functions. Whereas Wisdom and Courage are more individual virtues.

What they are getting at is that whether or not we think about it, or accept it, reality is inherently and inescapably social. The natural and human worlds are a community of tasks, needs, interests, differentiated functions. Ethical egoism and atomism are simply not the Way Things Are. So Lao Tzu is not being a hopeless idealist or Utopian in suggesting to us that "To be fair is to share the whole/ And so enlarge one's world." (III, 67, 3) In this light, bootstrap individualism is a cunning deception. We are not speaking here of the details of political ideology. Rather the idea is that exclusiveness and injustice are born of the biases, illusions, and tricks of individual and collective ego. The noble myth of the kinship of all people is in fact the highest and most basic truth. It is at once the spiritual destiny and practical necessity of the earth as a single community.

The quality and value of **CHIEN** is therefore a principle of Justice as planetary ecology in the most radical sense. But its full realization is contingent upon each individual, household, village, province, and nation taking it to heart and putting it into action:

> Thus is each dimension measured
> In its own domain,
> Person by person,

> Clan by clan,
> Town by town,
> Nation by nation,
> And the world, too,
> In its encompassing sphere. (III, 54, 3)

One way or another nature will balance accounts, and the haves and havenots get what they deserve in the long run.

> Being rich without sharing
> Diminishes one's world. (III, 67, 4)

> Halls filled full
> With guns and gold
> Have no defense.
> So pride of wealth
> Brings on its own misfortune. (I, 9, 3,4)

War and internal strife are avoided or at least reduced by the attainment of social justice and a working harmony among neighbors at all levels. Lao Tzu's advice to the ruler is this: Conduct the channels of power with a gentle and generous heart:

> Weal and woe take their turns
> On fortune's road—
> Each leading on and
> Hiding from the other.
> Who knows this circle's end!
> When exceptions become the rule
> And evil measures out the good,
> Confusion reigns among the people.

How does a sage set right
A world on end?
By being
Just but not fierce,
Frugal without cutting corners,
Direct but not blunt.
The sage has the light
To show the Way
Without self-glory. (II, 58, 2,3)

The crux of the problem is the common, simple, and ultimate case of mistaken identity. It is our inveterate tendency to limit the image of ourselves to our bodily frame and the ego's claim to glory in the shadowplay of life's stage. The enlightened self looks within and sees beyond and so naturally regains the wider life that aggressive souls would take by force. We have encountered this wisdom before in our journey among the symbols along the Way. Lao Tzu refocuses the problem and its resolution through the treasured quality of HOU, or Humility.

The image presented in the character conveys the appropriate comportment in travelling on life's Way. The symbol on the left means to march in step, or generally, to go. Above on the right is a fine thread suggesting "gentle;" and below it the root, "to follow." The pictogram extends to its common meanings as "coming after, heritage, and posterity." Thus it carries with it the central idea of putting others first. Lao Tzu's no-nonsense advice invites us to displace the ego as the exclusive or primary center of our lives:

To be humble leaves an open place
For others while saving room for growth.
Whereas being first in line

Is a lonely and third rate space indeed! (III, 67, 3,4)

In the positive turns on the wheel of fortune, we foolishly would take credit, and are often ungrateful for the conspiracy of chance and the support of the community. For the negative twists of fate, we curse the stars, work ourselves into a shrill pitch of high anxiety:

> In or out of grace, Beware!
> As a fortune made or missed
> Is largely ego's trick.
> Just what are these fateful
> Graces, good or bad?
> For services rendered often rue
> The favored more than those denied.
> Again, beware of both.
> So what is meant by saying
> These inflated goods and empty griefs
> Are ego's game?
> Just that our greatest cares are born
> Of a small possessive self.
> So rise above yourself—
> Be free of worry and woe! (III, 13, 1,2)

It is a question of vanity in its deeper aspect rather than on the less serious side which is concern with mere appearances. Lao Tzu puts the spotlight on the folly of ego's inflated self-importance. It is indeed a "fool's vain show:"

> Those who take themselves
> Too seriously tend to
> Overreach and topple,

Overbear and stumble,
Showing off the dark and dreary
Play in which they live.
Such bravado hides
An ugly life—
A braggart thinly masking
An empty part,
A stand-in crying over
Missed chances. (Ill, 24, 1,2)

This absurd charade is a colossal case of miscasting. One must learn to appreciate and identify oneself with the whole play, support and savor each part, assume the roles that fit one best or are needed in a pinch for the scene at hand. The smaller the actor's ego becomes, the larger the self expands, 'til one is in harmony with the whole work and play of life, whatever it brings along the Way. It is the "lowly road to the higher Good:"

Great rivers and seas prevail
Over the waters of the earth
Because they gather in
The lowest places in the land
As all currents are naturally
Drawn to them.
So sages preside over people
With humble speech,
Provide for others
Putting self behind. (I, 66, 1,2)

Although the essence of Humility and the openness of self it entails means putting others first, it does not necessarily require taking the bit parts or supporting roles in the drama of social and political reality. In fact the way of the humble is perhaps more important for those at the top of the power pyramid. Realizing this, Lao Tzu has a number of poems concerning this prerequisite quality for sagely rule. The entire Second Part of this edition is devoted to the Way to conduct power when in positions of authority. Recalling the passage just quoted above where the Taoist sage draws on the grand metaphor of earth as a vast reservoir in undiminished supply and in endless cycle, see now how the poet can shift from the water image to earth, stone, and soil symbols to underline the irrelevance of honor and glory in their vain outward show:

> Nobility is rooted
> In common clay.
> The exalted have the humble
> As their foundation.
> What's behind the mask
> The world's worthies wear—
> Affecting peasant roots,
> Rubbing shoulders with the masses?
> What good is the carriage of state
> Without its wheel?
> Respectability still bears
> The jangle of jade
> Where humility prefers
> The sound of simpler stones. (II, 39, 4,5)

Having measured out and assayed the qualities of Justness and Humility as sharing the world and opening the self, we now take up the final and central Treasure in Lao Tzu's threefold philosophy of

values. It is important to note that the quality of TZ'U, Love or
Caring, is presented first in the series of basic Goods, and in the
unfolding of the poem's insights the last and best quality to be
cherished. The Chinese character denotes the heart or feelings in
the lower part of the symbol, and lush vegetation spread above it.
TZ'U thus connotes fine, deep, and far reaching compassion. It is
tender loving care in its most extraordinary energy and extravagant
scope.

In the middle of this Poem of the Three Treasures the sage tells
us that "To care extends the heart/ And gives one courage to go
on." (III, 67, 3) The Latin roots of our word "magnanimous" carry
much of the virtue expressed by the Chinese TZ'U. Magnanimity is
literally "greatness of soul", expansiveness of heart. Like luxuriant
vegetation growing and pervading its immediate region, loving care
radiates out from a personal center and embraces all it encounters.
What is remarkable in the passage just quoted is the connection
between spiritual compassion and courage. The universal compass
of such love empowers the self to face the changes, patterns, and
forces that comprise one's world with gentle but firm confidence. It
is essentially a trust in the rightness of accepting each thing for
what it is and assisting its development, or at least leaving room for
its growth. Love means allowing things to become what they truly
are.

The common alternative to loving as confidence and courage is
a brash and aggressive assertion of one's will. It seeks and revels in
the politics of resistance: "Being bold without caring/ Is simply
reckless." (III, 67, 4) Tending the garden of one's life with love
means taking care, taking time to meet, appreciate, and largely let
what grows in its own turf flourish on its own terms: "Force the fruit
and hasten decay/ Push the river/ And be carried away!" (I, 30, 5) In
the normal interplay of vectors and forces, love's dynamics have the

tendency to want to do something for or to the beloved. But Lao Tzu advises us that the spiritually grounded Caring of TZ'U is a trust in a higher law and deeper spring of action. So the discipline in the art of loving is more in the direction of sparingness and selectivity. It tends the garden of its beloved by attending, cherishing, supporting, gently guiding. In essence it is nurture, the Mother, as we explored in Section Two of this Introduction. The misdirected passion and presumption of blind love is to know too well and yet too little the law of the other's life. So it is as true of personal relationships as of political strategies,

> Those who stand in nature's place
> In executing higher laws
> May find themselves
> Cut off along the way.
> The artless use of sharp devices
> Seldom yields but shreds and slices I (I, 74, 3,4)

Profound and genuine Love, then, encompasses trust, courage, letting be, patient and constant attending, openness, a discerning eye, a forgiving heart, and a sure and light touch. Lao Tzu is no sentimental romantic gliding along the path of love as a bed of roses. Love's connections can be a jungle of entangled feelings and wounded egos. Nevertheless, the counsel of the sage in sharing his Three Treasures as tools for living is that the combined qualities of Fairness and Humility centered in a loving heart is the only Way to go. The waywardness of the selfish, aggressive will inevitably brings its own fated and deserved reward:

> What need is there of death
> If we live like this?

Kindness in life's contest
Is the best defense
And wins over all.
For heaven is an ever-present guide
To those who walk
The Compassionate Way. (Ill, 67, 5)

VI. RETURNING TO THE WAY MEANS RECOVERING THE ROOTS OF PEACE

Our next meditation among the symbols of the Way To Peace quite literally brings us back full circle to the beginnings. It carries forth our thought not only to the commencement of our study but to the Primal Origin of things: the Way of Life itself. The theme of "returning to the source," "recovering one's roots," "restoring balance," appears again and again to call up the sense of unity and community. It points to the integrity and creative power of Being as parenting and providence, inheritance and reverence. Recalling our reflections on the Way as a nurturing Mother (see Section Two of this Introduction), we find Lao Tzu in Poem Forty presenting to us the whole cosmos as a single family:

> All creatures great and small
> Arise from the sphere
> Of concrete being;
> And this luminous orb of life
> Springs forth out of nothing
> But the Way. (IV, 40, 2)

What this means to us in the interplay of life's tasks and entertainments is living in the light of this community. It is not mere sagely practical advice but the deeper urge of Power that we let wide experience guide us in the uses of force and counterforce, the push and pull of life's complex energy systems. Very simply and directly, we are counseled:

> Recovering the Path
> Is the Way things work—

> Opening up and yielding
> Is how they come home to it. (IV, 40, I)

This image of homecoming is explicitly present in the structure of one of the three Chinese characters our Taoist poet uses for recovery or return. And it is the word Lao Tzu chooses somewhat more frequently. The pictogram FU describes on the left the form for walking or stepping. On the right above are the gates and walls of the city or fortifications. Under this is the root word for "follow" or "marching in file." Together these mean to return to quarters; or by extension, homecoming, or any process of going out and returning.

The second character employed by the sage is HOU, which we have already looked at as the third of the Three Treasures: Humility. It is by virtue of its component symbols that HOU is read as following or yielding as well as humility. Its clear connotation is letting others go first, following or deferring to those who know the path, or yielding outward position to those who blindly wander astray or not actively resisting those willful souls who insist on getting their own way. This is why HOU as humility and openness and yielding is an essential quality of the sage. You can never be thrown off track or lose your higher self if you are always at home in the journey of living. The world is at once your heritage, inheritance, personal responsibility, and family support system. It nurtures you and you in turn take care of it.

Lao Tzu, of course, radicalizes and extends this quality to its widest compass. You accept the world as it must accept your part in its games and tasks. Although everything ultimately returns and dissolves in the cosmic cycle in its necessary process, the third word for Return used by Lao Tzu indicates that for spiritual beings the meaning of self-recovery or homecoming is a conscious act. The character **FAN** depicts a hand in the act of turning something over. As an ethical and spiritual virtue it is a movement of will directed by farseeing vision and open, outreaching disposition of the heart.

In the passages which dwell in the image on Return we find several illuminating variations on the theme. As if to baffle or confuse us, though hopefully not to scare us away, the sagely trickster as trail guide of the Path would give us an obscure clue to the spiritually homeward bound:

> The luminous face of things
> Is veiled in mystery
> Yet its soul is clear and deep.
> It is the tale of a place
> Unspeakably vast
> Where all things
> Return to nothingness—
> A form that never appears—
> An image without a shape. (IV, 14, 3)

All metaphors and symbols finally break down in the face of reality. Travellers never "arrive" at home, for there is no end-of-the-line terminal, no final resting place. If it is a static peace we are looking for, we shall only tire ourselves chasing rainbows on a wild goose chase:

> The True Way
> Ever eludes us,
> Untouched by reaching hands.
> What's behind these probes
> Is indeed unsearchable.
> Yet whatever it is

That draws us beyond
Our grasp merges in
One creation. (IV, 14, 1,2)

If we are striving for Peace, longing for home, lost on our way, we need to stop looking. This is the place; we are already here. It is in the power and compass of our selves:

No need to pass your garden gate
To know the world,
Nor peer through windows
To see the Celestial Road.
The more you go out of your way
To travel, the less you see
Of essential living. (IV, 47, 1)

On the high and wild road of life's adventure a steady heart and a clear head will stand you in good stead if that centered clarity finds itself at one with the Eternal Eye and I of all the world:

Reach for the higher
Mountain places of your self
All calm and clear
And see
How all things flourish and return,
Each creature coming home
To recover its roots.
Recovering the root
Means just this:
The dynamics of peace
In being recalled to our common fate

In the kinship of all creation.
Knowing this eternal truth
One sees all things with
Extraordinary clarity—
Eternity's radiant light. (II, 16, 1-3)

Eternity is not some abstruse metaphysical or theological
notion, not some far-off place and time; it is Being Eternally Present
to the world as Mother. Each of us is at once Parent and Child. This
is how to "recover life's infinite reserve of spiritual power...[and]
that extraordinary freshness and fitness of a child." (II, 28, 2,1).
Thus Returning to the Root as the inner and outer dynamic of peace
is the key to a harmonious and abundant world. Unequivocally the
Taoist sage enjoins us to restore the health and blessing of a
bountiful life by tapping the depths of spiritual power pervading all
nature:

All life prospers when
The spirit of community
Returns to favor all
Who dwell in the Radiant Way. (II, 65, 2)

When nature's balance
Is the mother of a people,
They endure.
The tree of community
Deeply planted,
Growing strong,
Will stand forever
In the light of the Way. (II, 59, 4)

VII. CHUNG AS CENTERING: A QUESTION OF BALANCE

To the average western observer the Chinese mind and culture are baffling in many ways. The inveterate habit of embracing opposites and even apparent contradictions exasperates the logical bent of Aristotle's heirs. Even our mode of rendering Chinese philosophic concepts is cast in our own rubrics. The idea of CHUNG or holding the Center is a case in point. The Middle Way or attaining the Mean can suggest a middle-of-the-road aversion for extremes. But both the character and its metaphysical-ethical meaning go beyond this notion of moderation. The pictogram itself has a directness and simplicity inversely proportional to its ease of attainment. In fact it is nothing less than the basic task of life: to be centered in the Way and on the Path.

The concrete image drawn in the character is of an arrow shot through the center of a square target. The denotation is thus not a mean between extremes but reaching the core, the central, the essential. As a task for aiming and shooting, it is a measure of exactness or quality perfected. CHUNG is a pivotal center, a high degree of quality, all meanings drawn from the marking and balancing of a square or circle from its sides or circumference held in perfect equipoise. How easy and elegant an image it is, and how difficult to accomplish in real life! The targets are moving and changing in shape, the wind-speed, force, and direction are unpredictably variable, the arrow transforms itself on the way to the target, and the archer is on the move as well. Life is an amazing matrix and contest of powers, aims, motives, obstacles. In light of this confusing game, how do we steady our aim and keep on center? It's essentially a question of bias. Earlier we found this in reflecting on PU JEN, or impartiality and objectivity. Literally, PU JEN means avoiding partiality or special interest, taking equal interest, not leaning or favoring one thing over another. We discovered that true power flows outward in all directions. So paradoxically the key to centering is finding one's center of gravity outside of oneself, transcending one's ego bias:

> It is nature's Way
> To be unbiased—
> For the cosmic span
> Is like a bellows
> Producing power
> As it goes…
> Inner balance holding sway. (IV, 5, 1,2)

Reaching this dynamic state of balance, an inner and outer harmony cannot be forced or imposed. It is less a striving or pushing than an easing up and letting go. When we are not there, we know it; when we are there, we are beyond self-consciousness or needing to know it. The peace of holding the Middle Way has a naturalness, innocence, and unselfconsciousness about it much like a child's. So in expressing what it is like to walk one's path, inner balance holding sway, Lao Tzu shows us how "A Child's Grace Illumines the Way:"

> Blessed as a child are those
> Who hold life's natural power
> With an easy grace.
> Wild beasts won't seize them.
> Birds of prey stay clear
> And fly away.
> Though pliant of bone

And soft of muscle,
A child's grasp is firm.
Oblivious to gender
Its vital energy can
Grow to perfection.
Crying and sobbing all day
Without getting hoarse,
A babe keeps its own kind of balance.
And lives in a world
Complete in itself.
To reach this child-like harmony
Is to recover life's extraordinariness
With radiant clarity. (III, 55, 1-3)

Thus centered power means free and open channeling of the environing forces flowing through one's being. The organism is a monitor and moderator of the streams of influence and schemes of recurrence. The challenge and the trick is to change or conserve the patterns without going beyond one's limit. All sagely traditions agree on the Middle Way; for nothing succeeds for long on the path of excess:

Therefore, sages avoid
Extremes of passion—
Indeed, all indulgence of the self—
And pursue the good and simple life
Without extravagance. (I, 29, 3)

We can see now that the knack of centering is to become the perfect vessel of the world's amazing energy. Neither indulging nor resisting—perfectly empty and completely fulfilled. It is less of a mystery how sages abide in silence the endless wonders of the world:

> They master the gates of passion
> And guard the doors of expression.
> Their subtle powers
> Dull life's daggers,
> Unfasten fetters,
> Tone down the glare,
> And temper the pace of
> The fast-shuffling world.
> Such is how all things work together
> In the domain of wisdom.
> Beyond the reach of
> Love and hate,
> Gain or loss,
> Praise or blame,
> The Sagely Way becomes
> The measure of the world. (II, 56, 1-3)

VIII. THE WAY TO PEACE THROUGH YIELDING AND FLEXIBILITY: THE PATH OF ACTIVE NON-RESISTANCE

In our last reflection we found **CHUNG,** or balancing and centering, to be a useful metaphor for finding and maintaining our life's axis and direction amid the welter of forces as well as obstacles around us. If we follow the insights contained in this group of symbols of the Way of Peace, it should be clear that the most effective way of being and acting in the universe of things and events is more like the complex processes of the natural world. It is a balance of inward order, outward mutual adjustments of influence, working among the varied schemes of recurrence, and making the most of mere chance.

Lao Tzu provides us with another illuminating group of symbols to clarify and refine the quality of sagely action. The poet philosopher chooses water for its yielding and malleable character. He also selects the image of new growth of wood for its softness and pliability. In Poem Seventy-six Lao Tzu expands upon the observation that among living things new growth prevails in virtue of its softness, resiliency, flexibility, and adaptability. Young shoots flourish above and below ground by yielding and going around immovable objects:

> Life's companions are
> Gentle and yielding...
> The newly born
> Are soft and supple
> While the dead grow
> Quickly hard and rigid.
> All things when young

Are tender as grass
And pliant as a sapling.
But deathly age finds them
Brittle and dry. (Ill, 76, 2,I)

In the Orient bamboo has long been lauded and used for its possession of these virtues. The Chinese word-symbols in this passage are used together: JE and JOU. They picture, respectively: a mass of curly lamb's wool, and a tree below a spear. Although when used separately they are synonymous, and so together might seem redundant, the difference of nuance as a phrase can be rendered as soft and supple or tender and pliant. At any rate they connote the practical observation and insight that the forces of new growth and sustained vitality are more of a yin or receptive non-resisting strength than assertive or aggressive yang power.

The adjective the sage often employs is CHU, which means "twisted, crooked, or bent." Literally, the Chinese character describes a mouth, dish, or hollow below, and a jewel set in it. The whole configuration thus connotes the quality of assuming the shape of things as they are, or receiving them openly as they come to us. As we saw in the positive effect of Non-Being, Non-Action, the Void, Emptiness, [see Section Four], so hollowness or concavity is the preferred way amid the pressures of the world:

Yield and be whole.
Go round the circle,
Yet reach the middle too.
Be open and fulfilled;
Be weary but soon recover;
So sages embrace a singleness
Of purpose on their Way…

> Light of heart and hand
> Quite simply they succeed. (Ill, 22, 1,2)

We can't obtain fulfillment by insisting on it, straining, pushing, and grabbing for it. It comes softly and naturally by "wearing the quiet habit of inner truth." (Ill, 22, 2) In a similar vein the poet-sage suggests that the gentle and yielding not only survive and endure, they stay young as well:

> Unconcerned with fulfillment,
> Sages never overfill their day
> And flourish in gray old age
> Making life's late season
> More like spring. (Ill, 15, 4)

While it is interesting to note that the Taoist philosopher connects the way of yielding with wholeness, yet we find it impossible to say which comes first: togetherness in oneself, or harmony with the world. Drawing on the vast storehouse of Chinese proverbial wisdom, Lao Tzu quotes some old sayings that give us a portrait of the open and yielding life, which was quoted earlier in Section Four:

> Deliberate when wading winter streams,
> Careful of surrounding dangers,
> Reserved as a grateful guest,
> Yielding as melting ice,
> Simple and unassuming as uncarved wood,
> Open and obliging as a mountain vale... (Ill, 15, 2)

As Henry David Thoreau's entire life and work expresses it, there is an exquisite kind of deliberateness in nature that operates on the near and far side of will, narrow desire, and near-sighted ego. For if it is your habit to "Find fault..."

> You will tend to fail yourself...
> To dwell on a moment's loss
> Is the self's indulgent blindness
> To the wider powers that be. (I, 23, 4)

Becoming one with life as it happens to you, attending to it with a light touch and a gentle heart is the true key to happiness:

> Seek life's wild finesse
> And become as deliberate
> And refined as creation's
> Simplest work. (I, 23, 3)

The philosopher of the Way is not oblivious to the negative side of human spirit which darkens the lives of billions of people and whole epochs of history. War and discord and suffering born of contentiousness or the will to domination are all too prevalent in our world. The answer that Lao Tzu, Thoreau, and Gandhi taught and lived is creative, peaceful non-resistance. The simple formula is to make no direct or violent contest in one's claims or demands. For in the path or wake of aggression and violent confrontation, "a bitter discontent remains to plague the powers that work for good...even if one could ease contending forces." (I, 79, I) Somehow the world needs to be persuaded that the non-aggressive Way of Peace as gentle, open, yielding is indeed more effective, more natural, and more truly human than the path of force and domination. The irony is that by giving up the offenses of selfish or nationalistic will to power, a person or nation gains a hundredfold in freedom and prosperity. This is why...

> The wise contend with nothing
> And go about their work
> Along the Way. (I, 81, 3)

> Yet somehow these sages
> Command a higher grace
> While bound to life's highest post.
> This paradox is
> In truth their fate. (I, 78, 4)

This wider good that could grace the earth is not the vain hope of an ancient Chinese mystic out of touch with history's stark reality. Lao Tzu insists that the accepted norm of power and the conventions of war and peace are a collective human delusion in violation of the creativity, harmony, and dynamic Peace that pervade the cosmic scheme of things. For "All in all, stillness is the norm" of nature's vast and patient Way. (I, 23, I)

Unfortunately, the sincere and direct appeal to common sense as well as to an ultimate self interest that encompasses the interests of others is most often lost upon the majority. For "the world finds this truth/ Too obvious to take to task." (I, 78, 3) Nevertheless, periodically the living Truth of Peace realizes itself as a vital possibility and promise hidden as an embryo in the womb of Nature. What would life be like in an enduring season of Peace? Our Taoist poet gives us a brief "Portrait of the People," a sketch around the symbol of water, Lao Tzu's favorite image of the TAO in nature, combined with the Way of the Sage as nurturing Mother.

This poem that rings the changes of a peaceful world concludes these "Jottings On the Way To Peace."

IN DUE SEASON

The Sagely Way
Serves like water,
Flowing beneath the fray
And skirting fault or blame.

When people, calm and
Deliberate as the turning sky,
Choose a solid house,
Compassionate thoughts,
Truthful words,
Competent rule,
They recover
A higher fitness
In all of life's affairs,
Attending to
Good timing with
The work at hand.

The highest good, Like water,
Will nourish all things
Without undue resistance.
It abides in places
Most folks shun,
As streams will flow unseen
And nearest to the common course—
So things run by nature. (III, 8, 3,2,1)

Index to original order of poems

ABOUT THE AUTHOR

Thomas Early is Associate Professor Emeritus at Humboldt State University. He taught in the Philosophy and Religious Studies Departments from 1971 to 2005. He earned a BA degree in philosophy and religion with honors from Hiram College in 1967. In 1972 at Boston College Graduate School he was awarded the doctorate Magna Cum Laude in philosophy with special emphasis in religious studies.

At present Dr. Early dwells in quasi-monastic retirement, within view of the Humboldt campus and the Pacific north coast beyond. His daily work in progress is to move smoothly from the world of academic multi-tasking to Parkinsonian mono-tasking to Taoist no tasking at all.